Fazlur Rahman Ansari
Aligarh Years: 1933 – 1947

Ahsan Academy of Research
Springs, South Africa

Fazlur Rahman Ansari
Aligarh Years: 1933 – 1947

Abdul Kader Choughley

Foreword by
Professor Abdur Raheem Kidwai

Tawasul International
Centre for Publishing, Research and Dialogue

First Edition 2021
Second Edition, 2024
ISBN: 978-81-952534-0-1
Abdul Kader Choughley

Ahsan Academy of Research (Springs, South Africa) akchoughley@gmail.com
www.ahsanacademy.co.za

SHELVCRAFT™
Shelving | Racking | Display | Shop Fitting Ph: 012 666 8933
Email: sales@shelvcraft.com
Website: www.shelvcraft.com

Published by
Tawasul International,
Centre for Publishing, Research and Dialogue

CONTENTS

Contents

Acknowledgements

Several people have provided much-needed help and support whilst I was busy writing this book. Mustafa Fazil Ansari: President of World Federation of Islamic Missions (Karachi) has been a source of inspiration for nearly a decade now, and I am grateful for his encouragement and on-going support. There are no words to describe my deep sense of appreciation to Professor Abdur Raheem Kidwai of Aligarh Muslim University (India) who has actively supported my literary activities. Under his mentorship and supervision, I have been able to develop a deeper understanding of Islamic revivalism in South Asia.

My wife, Muniera has been responsible for the technical production of our publications. Her unwavering support and encouragement in the completion of the manuscript is acknowledged. Adam Kolia, former editor of the popular *Ramadan Annual* (Durban) has been extremely helpful in providing articles relating to Dr Ansari's contribution to this esteemed magazine.

It has been more than twenty years since the first edition of *Islam to the Modern Mind* which was edited by Yasien Mohamed was published in 1999. The study on the eminent scholar, Dr Mawlana Fazlur Rahman Ansari was inspired by Anver Essa of Shelvcraft (South Africa). His profound admiration of this prominent figure in Islamic resurgence culminated in a number of books which he singlehandedly published. Several editions with a print run of ten thousand copies were distributed at no cost to individuals, academics, universities and organisations in many parts of the world. This was a mammoth task which Anver meticulously carried out. It will be no exaggeration to state that his publishing efforts on Dr Ansari and Mawlana Abdul Aleem Siddiqui are unsurpassed. To date, eight books of exceptional scholarly merit have been brought out and are indispensable reference works on the Islamic reformist thought in South Asia.

Anver has consistently maintained a low-key profile; his unassuming personality and passionate commitment to Islamic studies are his outstanding traits. His ambitious plans to extend the scope of academic research are illustrative of his vision to promoting Islamic scholarship.

May Allah bless his efforts.

Fazlur Rahman Ansari Timeline: 1914-1947

1914-Born on 19 August 1914 in Muzzafarnagar to a distinguished family who traced their lineage to the illustrious *Sahrbi*, Khālid Abu Ayyub Ansari.

1918- Commenced *hifdh al-Qur'ān*.

1924 - Pursued *Dars i-Nizāmi* in Meerut.

- Enrolled at Meerut College to study English.

1931 - Contributed articles for the following newspapers:

-*Muslim Standard of Ceylon*

-*Royal Islam of Singapore*

1932 – First meeting with Mawlana Abdul Aleem Siddiqui at Meerut College.

-Wrote his debut book *The Beacon Light* in refutation of Christian polemics against Islam.

1933 – Completed *Dars i-Nizāmi* course in Madrasah Islāmia (Meerut).

-Enrolled at AMU for a BA degree.

-Wrote his second work, *Christianity at the Crossroads*.

1935 – Obtained the prestigious award in recognition of his outstanding achievement in his BA and BSc degrees respectively.

-Received the coveted gold medal for establishing a new record in Philosophy (98%).

-Awarded the *Haqqi* prize in recognition of his mastery over Arabic in the B.A. examinations.

-Wrote the following monographs:

A New Muslim World in Making.

Islam in Europe and America.

1936 – Studied the post-*Dars i-Nizāmi* course under Professor Sayyid Sulayman Ashraf in the Sunni Theology Department.

-Wrote *Muhammad The Glory of the Ages.*

1937 – Deputed by Mawlana Siddiqui to work in Singapore to counter anti-Islamic propaganda.

-Was editor of *Genuine Islam* magazine.

Co-ordinated the All Malaya Missionary Society.

-Wrote *Trends in Christianity.*

1938 – Major contributions in defending Islamic law from the media, in particular *Straits Times* of Singapore.

1939 – Selected as a Fellow to pursue post-graduate studies in Germany.

1940 – Wrote *Islam and Christianity in the Modern World.* 1941 – Completed the Bachelor of Theology (BTh) course.

1942 – Completed his M A in Philosophy with meritorious achievement: First Class First.

-Elected president of Philosophical Society of AMU.

-Studied another MA which included subjects like Politics, Economics and Comparative Religions.

-Commenced his PhD in Philosophy under Syed Zafarul Hasan.

1944 – Appointed member of Education Planning Committee mandated by Muhammad Ali Jinnah.

-Published his *The Present Crisis in Islam and our Future Educational Programme.*

1945 – Contributed a series of articles on Communism which was published as *Communist Challenge to Islam* in 1951.

1947 – Could not submit his doctoral dissertation after Syed Zafarul Hasan migrated to Pakistan.

-Copy of his dissertation destroyed during Partition of India.

-Accompanied Mawlana Siddiqui along with his family to Pakistan.

-Worked as private secretary to Mawlana Siddiqui in his tabligh work.

Foreword

Dr Abdul Kader Choughley, a brilliant scholar with several valuable studies on Islam in South Asia, with the focus on Islamic Revivalism, deserves accolades for his yet another insightful, analytical work on Fazlur Rahman Ansari (1914-1974), a worthy Islamic scholar and activist. While Dr Choughley's earlier work *Fazlur Rahman Ansari: Life and Thought* (2012) provides a helpful overview of Ansari's illustrious accomplishments in the cause of Islam, the present study focuses on his formative years, 1933- 1947, especially his intellectual development as a student of Philosophy at the Aligarh Muslim University, Aligarh, India. On reading this book, readers gain good acquaintance with Ansari's worth-emulating oeuvre. For this remarkable feat Dr Choughley is to be complimented.

Divided into 7 Chapters, this study first places Ansari in the broader academic context of the day, particularly the influence of Abdul Aleem Siddiqui (1892-1954), the Islamic *dāʻī* par excellence, and of the Aligarh Muslim University, a great seat of Oriental learning and Muslim culture, on the supple mind of only 19 years old Ansari in his quest for knowledge. Professor Syed Sulayman Ashraf, Dept of Theology and Professor Zafarul Hasan, Dept of Philosophy, in their own ways, opened up new vistas of scholarship and interpretation for him. Under the spell of the inspiring teachings and the role model of Mawlana Abdul Aleem Siddiqui, the young Ansari resolved to devote his time energy, rather life to promoting Islam. At the young age of only 23 years he embarked upon tabligh (preaching mission) in Singapore. This proved to be an excellent training ground for his illustrious preaching career travels as was glibly described in the Western media wielded considerable influence concerning Islam's universal role. At the heart of Ansari's vision of tabligh was the synergy of knowledge and spirituality. The moral decline that had eroded religious consciousness could be attributed to the pervasive influence of materialism. Marxism, Communism and Capitalism were offshoots of the materialistic worldview that relegated the universal values of Islam to the margins. Shorn of apologia and polemics, Ansari presented a cogent critique on these ideological systems. In more than one way, they were deemed as existential threats for mankind. Likewise, his deep reflections on the flawed interpretations of religion in the main by philosophers and scientists spurred him to offer a rational interpretation of Islamic culture and civilisation. According to Ansari, revealed religion like Islam offered a shari`ah that was not time and culture specific. Rather, the mainstay of mankind's happiness lay in following the divine prescriptions as outlined by the Holy Prophet (SAW). The imprints of Syed Zafarul Hasan's erudition were visible in Ansari's cosmopolitan outlook on philosophical matters.

Two attributes set Ansari apart from his peers: research and reverence. His research output was remarkable as can be gleaned from his *Communist Challenge to Islam*. The references are extensive and are reflective of Ansari's historical acumen. Likewise, his monograph *Foundations of Faith* brings in different dimensions of philosophical thought. These works are well-structured and bear the hallmarks of enviable scholarship. Apart from his spiritual affiliation with Mawlana Siddiqui, Ansari held in high esteem scholars like Sayyid Sulayman Nadwi and Mawlana Abdul Majid Daryabadi. His correspondence with and reliance on their scholarly contributions mark his sense of reverence. Unassuming in his ways and dyed in the Islamic tradition of *adab* (decorum), Ansari embodied the ideals of the *iqrā* model. In a particular sense, AMU created the academic ambience for brilliant scholars like Ansari to grow and nurture their potentials in the cause of Islam.

Dr Choughley has explored energetically and effectively Ansari's service to the promotion of Islam in various parts of the world. So doing, he has presented before readers a larger picture and a wider context, as for example, the status of Islam/Muslims in the UK where Ansari carried out his Islamic mission, and the intellectual, ideological milieu of the day, then dominated by Communism. He has examined also the Christian faith and practice in the day, with an eye on elucidating Ansari's nuanced response to Communism and Christianity.

Likewise, in assessing Ansari's contribution to *sirah* studies, Dr Choughley surveys the 19th century *sirah* corpus, particularly Sir William Muir's obnoxious *Life of Mohammed*, and its befitting rejoinder, *Khutbat Ahmadiya* and its English version by Sir Syed Ahmad Khan. This is followed by Dr Choughley's critique on Ansari's cogent work, *Muhammad: The Glory of Ages* (1933), which pays a glowing tribute to the Prophet's multifaceted personality and his very many accomplishments. In the context of Ansari's global Islamic activism, Dr Choughley has pertinently analyzed the status of Islam in the Great Britain, which had received a highly welcome boost owing to the yeoman's services by these converts to Islam in the early 20th century: Lady Cobbold, Muhammad Marmaduke Pickthall who, at the behest of the Nizam of Hyderabad, India, brought out the first presentable English translation of the Quran in 1930, and Muhammad Asad whose perceptive writings protected the young modern Western educated Muslim across the world against the trappings of the Western culture.

As part of his *da'wah* (propagation of Islam drive) Ansari had to tackle the challenges posed by the aggressive Christian missionary work and the then formidable Communism, with its false hopes, particularly for the masses. Dr Choughley discusses well Ansari's strategies in countering these challenges. A gratifying and rewarding part of Dr Choughley's study is how Ansari drew upon the Islamic intellectual giant, Dr Muhammad Iqbal (d. 1938) which provided Ansari with plenty of food for thought for his grand Islamization of know ledge project, apart from raising his morale and reinvigorating him for articulating the message of Islam globally. Ansari's engagement with the science *versus* religion debate, raging in the early 20th century Muslim intellectual milieu, and his perception of the Islamic faith and practices have also been critically examined. This brings into sharper light the genius of Ansari. The two Appendices unravel much more about Ansari's attainments.

Dr Choughley's thorough grounding in the relevant scholarship is evident from both his copious annotations and his Bibliography. This book is destined to be used with immense profit by all those who are interested in Islamic revivalism and 20th century Islam in South Asia with a pointed reference to the stellar striving of Fazlur Rahman Ansari in the cause of Islam. May Allah shower His choicest blessings on both Ansari and Dr Choughley for their unflinching commitment to Islam and their sincerity of purpose.

Professor Abdur Raheem Kidwai
Director, K A Nizami Centre for Quranic Studies Aligarh Muslim University, Aligarh- Former Visiting Fellow, School of English University of Leicester, Leicester, UK

Preface

In his magnum opus, a masterpiece in its own right, a unique historic contribution to Islamic thought and Islamic Moral Philosophy - 'The Qur'anic Foundations and Structure of Muslim Society,' Dr Hafiz Muhammad Fazlur Rahman Ansari (ra) underscores the Quranic perspective of the essential attribute of the Integrated Individual. "Moreover he stands in special relationship with God in terms of the attribute of 'personality' which *both* possess and in consequence, his status among God's creatures is that of the vicegerent of God (II:30). He carries a responsibility on his shoulders which 'the heavens and the earth and the mountains' found themselves unable to bear (XXXIII:72). He has a cosmic mission... It is supra cosmic. For he belongs to God and unto Him he is journeying (II:156). As a vicegerent he should function as an integrated being, namely, comprehensively, harmoniously and creatively, in all dimensions of his personality: physical, spiritual, moral, intellectual and aesthetical."

On closer inspection and in retrospect, one finds the personality of Dr Ansari (ra) admirably projecting the attributes of greatness imbued in Islamic traditions, surpassing all the above criterion, setting new standards and excelling in each area in the domain of personality discernable from the record of his yesteryears and beyond in fulfillment of his supra cosmic mission. His disciplined and distinguished intellectual caliber is manifest during his entire life span which was full of outstanding achievements and exemplary performance in discharge of his obligations despite formidable odds and seemingly insurmountable difficulties he faced throughout his eventful life. The chronological enlistment so painstakingly constructed from archives by the esteemed author Dr Abdul Kader Choughley highlights the strength of Dr Ansari's conviction enthused by his enormous determination, zeal and utter devotion to his commitment which is optic throughout his academic and missionary career.

As a scholar and researcher he displayed an uncanny acumen, sagacity, foresight, indomitable spirit and enthusiastic diligence in tackling issues of far reaching consequence from his very inception in the field of scholarship. His earlier writings which date back to his teenage reveal his keen perception, depth of insight, objective and methodical approach to assess and resolve problematic issues. The critical intellectual appraisal of his contemporaries, in relation to his intellectual endeavors during his stay at the AMU speaks volumes about his promising abilities, and the sincerity of his commitment to meet the challenges, to review and resolve the queries posed by the modern mind questing knowledge to conform to the scientific thought and technological advancement of the age, a hallmark of the present century. As Poet Philosopher Allama Iqbal (ra) rightly states in his book – Reconstruction of Religious Thought in Islam: 'And religion, which in higher manifestations, is neither dogma, nor priesthood, nor ritual, can alone ethically prepare the modern man for the burden of great responsibility which the advancement of modern science necessarily involves and restore to him that attitude of faith which makes him capable of winning a personality here and retaining it hereafter'. One can see the unanimity of views between the two intellectual giants of this age.

As an erudite Islamic missionary he represented the true religion par excellence, for he had chosen a leadership role at a time when Islam was confronted with challenges from within the body politic of Islam and from without in the form of Communism on the one hand and its categorically opposite Capitalism on the other. Under the umbrella of British masters and as part of the insidious plan and in addition to the sectarian divides, Qadianis emerged in the Indian subcontinent designed to create confusion, dissent and division. Innocent minds were being misled by the Qadianis or Ahmadies - saplings of the British rule, and mischievous designs were perpetually hatched to divide the Muslim Ummah through nefarious means and create rift and differences aiming to thwart the principle of Unity (wehdet) among Muslims, the profound fundamental tenet of Islam which ensured unity of Ummah under a single banner.

Conscious of his responsibilities as a serious Islamic scholar, analyst and missionary, he drew the attention of the Ummah to this rising menace and the storm that was brewing through his discourses at the AMU and his comprehensive writings detailing the causes, their perilous socio religious impact on the generations to come and the remedial course of action to stem the tide. Dr Ansari was firmly convinced that proper education alone could develop the thought matrix of the Muslim minds and thwart and repulse the invasive, insidious and rife bigotry with which the Ummah was stricken. He voiced his concern on plethora of social ills emerging from the lack of proper understanding of the Quranic guidance in terms of individual and collective social responsibilities as Muslims. His writings show stupendous grasp of the historicity in relation to Man's journey of evolution. His understanding of science astonished even the great scientific minds of his age. His explanations of natural laws and their conformity with Quranic principles through science and philosophy were acclaimed far and wide as highly invigorating, enlightening and inspirational. Dr Choughley has aptly highlighted his efforts in the context of the dire need for Islamisation of contemporary knowledge and his efforts to synthesize and customize the process of education synchronizing it with the belief and value system of Islam.

His works as a reformist stands out in elucidating the intricacies of the wisdom of Quranic principles and the comprehensive emergent code of life in the modern day perspective and in keeping with the challenges of the current era. As a zealous upholder of dynamic orthodoxy in Islam, his discourses and his written works are the efflorescence of his genius.

Mere words would not suffice to express my deep appreciation of the assiduous research and stupendous efforts of the author in tracking the intellectual and spiritual progression of Dr Ansari during his academic and missionary sojourn at the AMU. The outstanding scholarship with which Dr Choughley charmingly describes the framework of Dr Ansari's thoughts reflected in his writings, simultaneously providing insight into the influence of his close association with his able mentors is commendable.

We owe a debt of gratitude to Dr Choughley for his meritorious contribution. May Allah bless him and all those who contributed in his noble venture in abundance with *His Blessings*. Aameen.

Mustafa F Ansari President
World Federation of Islamic Mission

Introduction

The early writings of Muhammad Fazlur Rahman Ansari (1934-55) are illustrative of his mastery over Islamic scholarship and the Western disciplines. At the age of eighteen he wrote his debut work, *The Beacon Light*, which was a collection of articles of scholarly merit. These articles addressed the issues facing the *ummah* during the first half of the twentieth century. The challenges which Ansari referred to in his subsequent writings included Marxism, Socialism and Capitalism. His trenchant criticism of these ideological systems stemmed from their respective pervasive influence on Muslim countries. In Ansari's view, Islam had to face a grave *fitna* (trial) which manifested itself in materialism - the worldview of Western civilisation. The grave consequences of these ideologies posed an existential threat to the spiritual dimensions embedded in the Islamic civilisation.

There are several strands which are interwoven into Ansari's multidimensional career that have given him fame as a scholar par excellence, *muballigh* and most importantly, an influential figure of Qur'anic studies. As a graduate of the Aligarh Muslim University (AMU), Ansari rose in prominence on account of his brilliant performance in his studies. It was in the academic environment of AMU that he not only developed a lasting rapport with his teachers but also wrote several works which were recognised for their original contributions in the field of Islamic studies. Ansari was considered a prodigy by the eminent scholars of the day on the following counts: 1) his career spanned Islamic and Western tradition and ii) his works were representative of contemporary Islamic thought.

The rise of Muslim modernism, a euphemism for liberal thought among the Muslim intelligentsia, made its presence in Muslim institutions like AMU. There were several reasons that were responsible for the growing disenchantment by the educated class with Islam as a way of life (*din*). It is a historical fact that British colonialism had implanted the culture of inferiority complex in the minds of the colonised Muslims through its technological advancement. As a result, the loss of faith seeped into the mindset of these modernist Muslims who advocated an unfettered interpretation of the foundational sources of Islam. This approach was fraught with manifold challenges, in particular Muslims' unwavering faith in Islam as a civilisational force. The changing geopolitics was another factor that weakened the unified presence of Islam. In this historical context, the Indian subcontinent underwent major political transformation and Muslims were compelled by circumstances to assert their Islamic identity amid the growing Islamophobic tendencies along religious lines.

The Orientalist project supported by British colonialism harboured an ingrained hostility against the Holy Prophet (SAW). Their scholarly research, in general, was built around the elements of fiction to malign the noble personality of the Holy Prophet (SAW). Needless to add, their production of literary works were distorted versions of biographical accounts drawn from the *sirah* sources. Entrenched prejudice, bigotry and polemics were common characteristics that were passed off as academic pursuits. In counter response, Ansari penned a biographical account by drawing upon Western scholarship to portray the Holy Prophet's role as the greatest model for mankind. In a similar vein, the well-documented articles were written in Western magazines, which were a testament to Ansari's deep learning and competence in *sirah* writing.

A pre-eminent scholar and *muballigh*, Mawlana Abdul Aleem Siddiqui (d. 1954), was also known as the roving ambassador of peace. His international tabligh journeys are his singular contributions to Islamic renewal. A meeting of minds in Meerut in 1932 between Mawlana Siddiqui and Ansari was the turning point to the latter's commitment to tabligh and the reconstruction of Islamic reformist thought. If AMU created the congenial environment for profiling Ansari's intellectual acumen, it was Mawlana Siddiqui who strengthened his spiritual training, an amalgam of values that would prepare him for his distinguished career in the years ahead. The tabligh travels are a snapshot record of the kindred spirit shared by these influential figures to promote the cause of Islam, and spread the Word of God among faith-based communities across the world.

It is a truism that Ansari, by virtue of his assiduous study of comparative religions, represented the Muslim voice to critique Christianity in terms of its deviant beliefs. No different was his scholarly approach to expose the hollowness of religious claims by the founder of Qadianism, who undermined the Finality of Prophethood. All in all, Ansari was able to demonstrate Islam's growing presence among converts in Europe and the United States of America, who in turn contributed richly to the dissemination of Islam. In this respect, Ansari's tabligh activism at a different level together with his scholarly reputation was the marker of the social cohesion taking place on the indigenous soil of the West. In the realm of the Islam and the West discourse, Ansari made pointed reference to the absence of spiritual values that had created blind spots by the Western civilisation's intrusive influence. Shorn of the *wahy*-inspired values, truth and wisdom, materialism has dominated the lives of people who no longer believe in the Afterlife. The pandemic of worldliness is elucidated by Ansari as a recurrent theme of his excellent works.

A timeline of events pertaining to Ansari's academic life underscores his well-defined response to the need for overhauling the Islamic educational system. His formulation of Islamic education harmonised with the *iqrā* paradigm, was in keeping with the Islamic ethos of centuries-long intellectual tradition. Interestingly, these works were written at a time when the demand for Pakistan under the leadership of

Muhammad Ali Jinnah was taking a definite shape and assuming greater importance in the political landscape of the subcontinent.

Clarity of vision is a hallmark of Ansari's brilliant exposition of the prevalent ideological systems and its impact on Muslim countries. His series of works dealing with the Communist menace is ranked among the finest pieces of writings which have exposed its pernicious consequences on the existing world order. Likewise, he ably highlights the failings of Capitalism which, too, has created the narrative of economic prosperity and the illusory spectre of universal democratic values.

The present study aims to document the formative influences on the multidimensional career of Ansari. Additionally, the role of AMU as the prestigious site of learning and the mentoring presence of Mawlana Siddiqui are examined in the context of Ansari's early writings (1933-47). It is hoped the study will add fresh insights into the life and thought of this illustrious scholar whose literary contributions have made a definite mark in Qur'anic studies.

Abdul Kader Choughley (Springs, South Africa)
30 March 2021
akchoughley@gmail.com

CHAPTER 1

Academic Profile of Fazlur Rahman Ansari

The chapter seeks to examine the academic profile of Fazlur Rahman Ansari during the period 1933-47. His biographical details have been comprehensively covered with particular reference to his tabligh vision in a contextual setting.[1] The formative factors which nurtured his formulation of the *iqrā* paradigm or holistic education are explored in the light of his contributions to Islamic reformist thought in the twentieth century.[2] It would be worthwhile to provide an overview of the patterns of Islamic learning which had shaped the intellectual tradition in the subcontinent.

Dars i-Nizāmi: An Assessment

Madrasah Islamia, Meerut offered the traditional *Dars i-Nizāmi* course which Ansari successfully completed in 1933. He initially enrolled as a part-time student in 1921 at the institution and always stood out as a student of exceptional ability and accomplishment. His versatility enabled him to pursue several courses (in many instances unrelated courses) concurrently and independently.[3] It was his stoic spirit and indomitable determination that spurred him to levels of academic excellence.

In South Asia, the *Dars i-Nizāmi* exemplified the evolution of Islamic learning over the centuries. It was the `ulama of Farangi Mahal (Lucknow) who were instrumental in devising

---

[1] Abdul Kader Choughley, *Fazlur Rahman Ansari: Life and Though,* (Springs, 2012).

[2] Ibid., 115-6.

[3] Khalil Rāna, *Tadhkirah 'Allāmah Fazlur Rahman Ansari al-Qādri,* (Lahore, 1992), 4-6.

the course which retained the Perso-Islamic culture in India. During the early eighteenth century, the *Dars i-Nizāmi* became the "dominant system of Indian Muslim education until it was overcome by the twin forces of Islamic reform and Western education in the twentieth century."[4] While Shah Waliyullah (d. 1762) envisaged a comprehensive study of the Qur'an and hadith to the contextualised understanding of *tajdid*,[5] the *Dars i-Nizāmi* reflected a different emphasis in Islamic scholarship: the rationalist sciences (*ma'qulāt*) like logic and *kalām* (scholastic theology) bore unmissable traces of Greek and Indian philosophy which were developed over the centuries by Muslim philosophers. The rationale for this approach was to encourage students "to think rather than merely to learn by rote syllabus ... to get to the heart of the matter, to present argument and to be flexible in their approach to jurisprudence (*Fiqh*)."[6]

Notwithstanding the relative success the *Dars i-Nizāmi* enjoyed in its initial years of implementation, the reformist (*islāhi*) trends associated with the Waliyullah tradition modified the syllabus and restored the primacy of the Qur'ān and sunnah as perennial sources of the shari'ah. In the twentieth century, bold steps were taken by several Islamic institutions to introduce modern subjects in their curriculum. English, stigmatised by the 'ulama largely because of British colonial rule in India, was gradually incorporated into the syllabus, not without fiery debates and the barrage of *fatāwā* against this decision. In a similar vein, agitational politics characterised the responses to modern education

---

[4] Francis Robinson, *Islam, South Asia and the West* (New Delhi, 2007). 67-72.

[5] The contributions of Shah Waliyullah to the reformulation of the Islamic sciences (*'ulum*) within the framework of *tajdid* and *ijtihād* have had an enduring impact in South Asia. See Muhammad Ghazali, *The Socio-Political Thought of Shah Wali Allah* (Islamabad, 2001).

[6] The emphasis of rationalism (*ma'qulāt*) in the *Dars i-Nizāmi* curriculum is examined in Francis Robinson, *The 'Ulama of Farangi Mahall and Islamic Culture in South Asia* (Delhi, 2000), 14-15, 32-7.

Academic Profile of Fazlur Rahman Ansari

rather than pragmatism, which otherwise could have turned the tide of both Islamic modernism and the Western culture in the subcontinent.[7]

Against the backdrop of the changing landscapes both in India and other Muslim countries, Ansari's involvement with education - Islamic and secular - must be examined. The *Dars i-Nizāmi* equipped him with consummate skills to explore the role of Islam in a rapidly changing world. Ansari acquired proficiency in Arabic and Persian to gain a deeper understanding of the sources of Islamic authenticity. Alongside his study of the traditional *'ulum*, he enrolled at Meerut College to pursue his studies in English as early as 1924.[8] His successful completion of the *Dars i-Nizāmi* with exceptional distinction and passing the Intermediate Science course at Meerut College opened up pathways of educational opportunities and enabled him to establish his academic credentials.

Meerut stood at the crossroad of change. Progressive Islamic ideas were embodied with the rise of modern institutions which attempted to build bridges with the *madāris*. In this regard, the Muslim elites of the city saw the colleges as the alternative to the forces of conservatism that held back Muslims in their quest of building a viable society.

Mawlana Abdul Aleem Siddiqui:
Roving Ambassador of Islam

An embodiment tabligh-in-action, Mawlana Abdul Aleem Siddiqui was an Islamic scholar whose contributions to the reconstruction of Muslim societies around the world have

---

[7] The conflicting responses to modern education have been comprehensively covered in Muhammad Qasim Zaman, *The 'Ulama in Contemporary Islam: Custodians of Change* (Princeton, 2002).

[8] *The Minaret* (Karachi, 1974),14

been documented in recent publications.[9] His reformulation of tabligh is his abiding legacy.

Ansari's first meeting with Mawlana Siddiqui was a life-turning experience for him. A strong bond of love developed between these two influential Islamic figures. The relationship reflected their respective Islamic and Western educational backgrounds. Mawlana Siddiqui was eminently suited to hone Ansari's academic skills for the purpose of tabligh. Moreover, in the company of the erudite scholar he was inducted into the realms of *tasawwuf*. This unique combination of *ta'lim* (education), tabligh and *tasawwuf* provided Ansari with renewed vigour to serve the cause of Islam. Under Mawlana Siddiqui's mentorship Ansari was entrusted with the responsibilities of replying to some of the latter's correspondence and contributing articles to magazines, etc. All in all, these pieces of writings largely focused on Islamic missionary journalism.[10]

Major Contributions

Wherever Mawlana Siddiqui went, both laymen and intellectuals among non-Muslims were inspired to enter the fold of Islam through his inspiring lectures. He wrote about twenty books in Arabic, Urdu and English. Likewise, he took an interest in world politics generally and Muslim politics particularly. On his own initiative he advocated the cause of Pakistan in the Arab world and other Muslim countries.

He moved for the elimination of the unjust imposition of the *hajj* tax, which the Saudi government reduced after protracted negotiation.

---

[9] Abdul Kader Choughley, *Abdul Aleem Siddiqui and His Mission* (Springs, 2013). Cf. Ibrahim Alladin, *Maulana Abdul Aleem Siddiqui: His Life, Thoughts and Message* (Curepipe, 2019).

[10] *The Muslim Digest*, January: 1965, 56-7.

Academic Profile of Fazlur Rahman Ansari

Mawlana Siddiqui's mastery over several languages lent charm and beauty to his thoughts and ideas. His eloquence was evident in his lectures before such learned societies as the Royal Asiatic Society of Shanghai (China) and the Oriental Culture Society of Japan, as well as during his lecture travels in the African continent. Whether on the public platform or in private conversation, Mawlana Siddiqui's exposition of contemporary problems was invariably marked by such lucidity, profundity and spiritual dynamism which was unrivalled among his peers. Broadly speaking, he belonged to both the worlds - traditional and modern; he was equally well-acquainted about the past, the present and the future; and he was equally impressive among the conservatives and the modernists. He was traditional in the sense that he carried on his venerable shoulders the responsibility and the obligation of delivering to humanity the message which Allah granted to the Messengers in the different parts of the world. At the same time, he was modern in the sense that he possessed the ability to expound the Islamic message in contemporary idiom. He believed that science and religion, far from being antagonistic, are complementary to each other and can be optimally pursued in the best interest of mankind.

In sum, Mawlana Siddiqui's tabligh vision transcended the traditional understanding of this term. In this respect, his missionary spirit focused on the unity of the Muslim *ummah* which regrettably was fragmented into sectarian groupings. Disunity had weakened the spirit of brotherhood *(ukhuwwah)* which Islam conceived as the bedrock of its universal message. For forty years he strove to promote the idea that the unity of the *ummah* embedded in the primary sources of Islam was the benchmark of Muslim progress across the world.

For forty years Mawlana Siddiqui's travels extended to major countries of the world. The modes of travels were hazardous in several countries especially in Africa which were under colonial rule. Flights between India and European countries including United States were in their initial stages; however, perseverance was his inner strength which he drew upon from the Qur'an and the prophetic model. Ansari's poignant remarks about Mawlana Siddiqui's spirit of resilience are revealing:

With no organised financial backing, with apparently unsurmountable difficulties constantly facing him, with broken health and continuous illness and with many to criticise and few to co-operate, he had to tread this lonely path. Under these adverse conditions, he maintained an admirable composure which imparted a spiritual glow to his every action. With his battle-cry: *"Back to the Qur'ān and the sunnah,* his watchword: *the unity of Islam"* and his conviction that *"[the] more religious Muslims become, the better will they succeed in solving all their problems,"* he fought against the forces of disruption and disintegration, creating harmony between the forces of conservatism, sectarianism and modernism.

In the wake of his endeavours came a new awakening, a fresh consciousness and a stronger will to work, and these factors resulted in the establishment of missionary societies, youth movements, organisations of the `ulama, educational institutions, mosques, orphanages, magazines and newspapers. And this new awakening captured the minds of all classes of Muslim society. Before the greatness of his work as also of his personality bowed princes and governors, judges and lawyers, students and professors, business magnates and bureaucrats and professionals from diverse backgrounds. His disciples in the 1950s exceeded nearly one hundred thousand souls while his admirers and friends numbered by the millions.[11]

---

[11] Choughley, *Abdul Aleem Siddiqui,* 31-3.

Academic Profile of Fazlur Rahman Ansari

In 1932 when Ansari was only eighteen years he wrote *The Beacon Light,* a first class missionary book on Islam and much earlier he started writing for Ceylon's (Sri Lanka), *Muslim Standard* and Singapore's *Real Islam.* Mawlana Siddiqui's pressing tabligh engagements did not give him sufficient time to respond to the spate of anti-Islamic literature published by Christian missionaries in Singapore. Polemical works denigrating Islamic teachings and the personality of the Holy Prophet (SAW) continued unabated, and no doubt, there was an orchestrated campaign to thwart tabligh activities among Muslims. Mawlana Siddiqui's role was two-pronged: to promote the universal values of Islam in Singapore and create a forum for inter-faith dialogue.

The Beacon Light, the seminal work of Ansari, was a refutation of the missionary's tirade against Islam. It was he who volunteered to write a monograph in defense of the Islamic teachings. In a short period of four hours the monograph was completed and in the words of an international law specialist it was a flawless piece of work.[12] Needless to add, the imprints of his mentor's training (*murabbi*) were very much in evidence. Ansari's academic debut was soon followed by his initiation into *tasawwuf.* The world of Islamic spirituality opened up before him through his association with Mawlana Siddiqui. In a particular sense, his intellectual horizon was broadened while his spiritual stature raised opportunities for his future tabligh role. Thus his contributions must be examined in the light of Mawlana Siddiqui's pioneering role during this formative period.

---

[12] *The Minaret,* January - February 1984, 17. Cf. Abu Abdul Quddus Muhammad Yahya, *Uhd i-Sāz Shakhsiyyat. Haidh Dr. Muhammad Fazlur Rahman Al-Ansāri Al-Qādri* (Karachi, 2018), 78.

Aligarh Muslim University (AMU)

The establishment of the Muhammadan Anglo Oriental College (MAO) in 1875 was a vision of the time and in the words of Sayyid Ahmad Khan "was to be a Muslim university on the model of Oxford and Cambridge universities which we have seen."[13] He advocated new trends which signalled a bold departure from the traditional Islamic curriculum.[14] According to Sayyid Ahmad, it was only after the 1857 uprising against British rule that the Indian Muslim community had realised the importance of learning Western sciences and English. In pursuance of this vision he founded various schools as well as a scientific society. Liberal sciences were given priority to the exclusion of technical sciences, which in fact held the key to the phenomenal rise of the Western powers in the world.

Sayyid Ahmad had witnessed the transformative power of these sciences during his visit to Britain in 1869.[15] Another drawback that prevented the educational reform of Sayyid Ahmad from exercising a positive influence on the Muslims of the subcontinent was the notable absence of a well-defined Islamic educational system that would keep it immune to the materialistic impulses of Western civilisation. Moreover, an integrated education system rooted in an Indo-Islamic milieu would have far-reaching consequences to alleviating the modern challenges Indian Muslims faced.

---

[13] Hadi Hussain, *Syed Ahmed Khan: Pioneer of Muslim Resurgence* (Lahore, 1970), 142.

[14] L.S. May, *The Evolution of Indo-Muslim thought after 1857* (Lahore, 1970), 39-40. Cf. Robert Ivermee, "The Aligarh Movement and the History of Colonial Education", in Abdur Raheem Kidwai (editor), *Sir Syed Ahmad Khan: Muslim Renaissance Man of India* (New Delhi, 2017), 102-3.

[15] In fact, his visit to England marked the beginning of his active career as an educationist, reformer and religious writer. See Hadi Hussain, *Syed Ahmed Khan*, 62-74. Cf. Kidwai, *Sir Syed Ahmad Khan*, 131-9.

Academic Profile of Fazlur Rahman Ansari

Keeping in mind Sayyid Ahmad's modernist leanings, his *Tafsir al-Qur'ān* (1886-1904) is succinctly described in these words:

> (Syed Ahmad) was not a trained theologian; his was essentially a restive soul seeking desperately some answer to the questions born of the spirit of his age, which had been agitating the minds of the Western educated Muslims. As a sincere, well- meaning Muslim, who apprehended breaches in the faith of the future generations of Muslims, he tried his hand at presenting a new version of Islam in which were somehow yoked together with the disparate notions of Deistic and Natural philosophy and articles of faith.[16]

Sayyid Ahmad argued that the Word of God must be in harmony with the Work of God. In other words, revelation (*wahy*) must not be in conflict with nature. This approach was clearly evident in his rational interpretation of the sacred text. Notwithstanding his modernist mindset, the establishment of the Islamic Theology Department (*Sunni*) during his lifetime was supervised by distinguished `ulama across the sectarian divide.[17]

Sayyid Ahmad's influence on the rising generation of Muslims was unparalleled in the social and educational history of Muslim India. The Aligarh Movement became the catalyst for the general diffusion of cultural and educational modernisation among Muslims. In many states of the subcontinent Muslims were inspired by its example to set up institutions which played a significant role in the evolution of

---

[16] Abdur Raheem Kidwai, "Qur'anic and Islamic Studies at the Aligarh Muslim University: An Assessment", in Juhi Gupta and Abdur Raheem Kidwai (editors), *Oxford of the East: Aligarh Muslim University 1920-2020* (New Delhi, 2020), 132.

[17] Ibid., 138-40.

the distinct Muslim entity.[18] The movement for the establishment of Aligarh Muslim University came into being in 1920. Khaliq Ahmad Nizami has also traced the evolution of the AMU from 1920 to 1945, after the death of Sayyid Ahmad in 1898 in his scholarly work.[19]

According to Sayyid Abul Hasan Ali Nadwi:

"[The] great Aligarh movement, whose destinies Sir Syed guided with conspicuous sincerity and ability for about half a century, was successful in a considerable way in filling the educational and economic void created in the Indian Muslim society with the collapse of the Mughal Empire and the establishment of the British rule. The movement gave to the community a fair number of highly accomplished young men, writers, thinkers, journalists and politicians, who spearheaded the Khilafat movement and played a role worthy of their glorious past in the national struggle for independence. Later, when the demand for a separate Muslims homeland was raised and the Muslim State of Pakistan came into being, the inspiration and guidance for it was provided mainly by the Muslim University of Aligarh."[20]

Viewed from the historical context, AMU developed into a prestigious institution in various disciplines and produced a generation of scholars with exemplary contributions. Ansari's stay at AMU was in line with the unbroken tradition of academic excellence.

---

[18] Sayyid Ahmad's influence on the formulation of educational and political theories which culminated in the establishment of Pakistan has been critically examined in Hafeez Malik, *Sir Sayyid Ahmed Khan and Muslim Modernisation in India and Pakistan* (Karachi, Royal Book Company, 1988).

[19] Khaliq Ahmad Nizami, *History of the Aligarh Muslim University* (Delhi, 1995).

[20] Abul Hasan Ali Nadwi, *Western Civilisation, Islam and Muslims* (Lucknow, 1974), 74-75

Ansari at Aligarh Muslim University: 1933-47

Ansari's prolonged study period at AMU (1933-47) may be divided into two phases. The first phase, 1933-7 saw his meteoric rise as a student of exceptional ability. His undergraduate studies - BA (Humanities), BSc (Science) and BTh (Islamic Theology) degrees attested to his academic brilliance. An eighteen-month hiatus (1937-8) inducted him into his first tabligh travel to Singapore. Thereafter, the second phase, 1939-47 brought him into prominence on two levels: his conceptualisation of Islamic Philosophy and Comparative Religion which he would develop in later years at Aleemiyah Institute; his writing output based on a wide range of contemporary issues. These periods brought him closer to Mawlana Siddiqui both intellectually and spiritually. There was no doubt that Mawlana Siddiqui's *faidh* (spiritual blessings) opened up opportunities which he derived from this companionship. Moreover, Ansari served as Mawlana Siddiqui's private secretary, a position which he held until the latter's death in 1954.[21]

Ansari joined the seat of Muslim learning and culture at AMU in 1933 and enrolled for the BA course. The subjects included in the curriculum were English literature, Philosophy, Theology, Arabic and Urdu. He graduated in 1935 with a First Class First. It was a remarkable feat for Ansari to pursue two degrees concurrently - BA and BSc for which he received the coveted gold medal. Another remarkable achievement enhanced his academic profile when he established a new record in Philosophy for obtaining **98% in Philosophy in the BA examination.** In addition to the prestigious awards, he received the *Haqqi* Prize for

---

[21] Yasien Mohamed, *Islam to the Modern Mind* (Paarl, 2006), 16

meritorious achievement in Arabic.[22] It must be noted that his undergraduate years were the preparatory period for his literary accomplishments at the institution.

Ansari also pursued a post-*Dars i-Nizāmi* course, Bachelor of Theology (BTh) under the eminent scholar, Professor Sayyid Muhammad Sulayman Ashraf (d. 1939), who was appointed lecturer in 1902 and later served as Chairman, Department of Muslim Theology. A graduate of the Madrassah Hanafiyyah in Jawnpur, Sayyid Sulayman possessed consummate skills in Arabic and Persian. His literary contributions in Arabic, in particular his compilation of the Arabic philology entitled *Al-Mubin* received critical acclaim from scholars like the noted Orientalist Browning and the Poet of the East, Muhammad Iqbal.[23] He also received a cash prize from the Indian Academy. His other work *Al- Anhār* written in Persian was considered a masterpiece by the literary critic and research scholar, Mawlana Habibur Rahman Sherwani (d. 1950),[24] whose own writings bear close affinity to the works of Sayyid Sulayman.[25]

Ansari studied tafsir, the last corpus of hadith literature, *'ilm-al-kalām* (scholastic theology) and *tasawwuf* under Sayyid Sulayman Ashraf. He paid tribute to his teacher from whom he acquired at the level of his higher education, knowledge of the Qur'ān and of the Islamic theological sciences.[26] Three

---

[22] *Mawlana Shah Hāidh Muhammad Fazlur Rahman Ansari*, 10. This paper was published by the Halqah Aleemia (Karachi).

[23] Cited in Hamid Ali Aleemi, *Muballigh i-Islam, Hadhrat 'Allāmah Muhammad Fazlur Rahman Ansari: Hayat wa Khidmāt* (Karachi, 2011), 20.

[24] Mawlana Sherwani held Sayyid Sulayman Ashraf in high esteem and their regular meetings at AMU mirrored their common academic interests and enduring association with the institution. For his biographical account, see Shams i-Tabriz Khan, *Sadr* Yar Jung, (Karachi, 1981).

[25] Sayyid Ashraf Sulayman held regular classes in tafsir at AMU for a number of years which were attended by students interested in advancing their studies of the Holy Qur'ān. On his obituary, see Sayyid Sulayman Nadwi, *Yād Raftagān* (Karachi, 1983), 189-91.

[26] Ansari, *The Qur'ānic Foundations and Structure of Muslim Society*, vol.1 (Karachi, 2012), xix.

important points emerge from Ansari's association with Sayyid Sulayman Ashraf. First, as a student he was able to master both classical and literary texts at an advanced level. Second, the degree he pursued was equivalent to the specialist study of the *'ulum* (disciplines) of the Qur'an and hadith. This required a comprehensive and analytical study of the primary sources of Islam. Ansari's profound understanding of these sources are respected in his various writings, including his major work *The Qur'ānic Foundations and Structure of Muslim Society*. Third, as a celebrated *sui*, Sayyid Sulayman Ashraf complemented, by his personal example, the fusion of shari`ah and *tasawwuf*. Like Mawlana Siddiqui's mentorship in the path of *tasawwuf*, Sayyid Sulayman's deep study of the classical texts had a profound impact on Ansari.

It would be worthwhile to examine Sayyid Sulayman Ashraf's vision of holistic education. Based on his thought-provoking writings which cover subjects like Arabic morphology, literature, philosophy, etc. his focus was on the reform of the Islamic curriculum. He argued that the sociopolitical circumstances prevailing in the country required a constructive approach to education. As much as there was stiff opposition from Dar al-'Ulums and Muslim political organisations against learning English and other 'secular' subjects, Sayyid Sulayman Ashraf countered this regressive attitude on two counts: i) Muslims were deprived of educational opportunities to make strides in their professional careers and ii) the Hindu majority were beneficiaries on account of their willingness to progress in all fields of learning.

Sayyid Sulayman Ashraf participated in several educational conferences which deliberated on the future educational prospects of Muslims. While he advocated educational reforms, he opposed any move that removed the primacy of the Islamic ethos in the curriculum. Like Iqbal, he deplored the tendency to separate Islamic and modern knowledge. It was at AMU that he gave shape and form to his interpretation of the *iqrā* framework, which in some limited ways produced positive outcomes.

Among his outstanding students were Fazlur Rahman Ansari, Dr Zakir Hussain (who later became President of India) and Burhan Ahmad Faruqi, the noted educationist who taught at the Aleemiyah Institute (Karachi).[27] After Ansari's graduation, Sayyid Sulayman Ashraf had an occasion to make the following remark:

> Rāfidh Fazlur-Rahman Ansari is a young man with a personality radiant with virtue and exceptional intelligence. As regards his academic distinctions, he holds a place of pride among the alumni of the Muslim University. He has studied the Islamic theological sciences for the most part under me, and has accomplished the task with industry and ability. In *tasawwuf* and philosophy too, he possesses an extraordinary interest and has studied certain classics in both the subjects from me. Islamic missionary work is his goal in life and I pray that Allah Almighty may bestow the choicest success on his labours in that field.[28]

A similar sentiment was echoed by Professor Abdul Aziz Memon, Chairman: Department of Arabic, concerning Ansari's versatility. He commented:

---

[27] Adapted from Muhammad Ahmed Tarazi and Mazher Hussain, "Proliferation and Significance of 'Modern' Contemporary Disciplines of Knowledge in the 20th Century: An Analytical Study of Syed Suleman Ashraf Bihari's Ideology", in *Al-Afkār* (2018), vol. 2:2, 109-28.

[28] *The Minaret*, 1974, 17 Cf. *'Ilān Min Jānib Halqah 'Aleemiyah Karachi bi Silsalah Intikhāb*, 11.

Academic Profile of Fazlur Rahman Ansari

I have not seen anyone who can equal him in gentleness of manners, excellence of character, love for knowledge, profoundness of concern for the important Islamic problems and courage for shouldering great tasks. Moreover, in spite of his young age, he does not stand below any seasoned elder in experience and executive ability... In short, I consider him capable of every good and great pursuit and fit to prove himself equal to any grand task that might be entrusted to him. *Hardly I have seen any student at this University who could excel or even equal him in his attainments which seldom combine in a single person.*[29]

Professor Abdul Aziz Memon (d. 1978) was an unrivalled scholar in Arabic literature. His critical editing of classical Arabic texts and his own publications on literary criticism surpassed works of Arabic literary figures like Taha Husayn (d. 1971).[30]

In recognition of his contribution to the Arabic language and literature he became a member of the esteemed academic institution[31] in Damascus. He was appointed a lecturer at AMU in 1929. He migrated to Pakistan in 1947 and was appointed Professor of Arabic in Karachi University. An accomplished scholar, he memorised almost a hundred thousand Arabic verses and had no peers in the Arab world.[32]

As mentioned elsewhere in the chapter, Ansari's exposure to

---

[29] See *Hāidh Shah Muhammad Fazlur Rahman Ansari*, 11.

[30] One of Taha Husayn's major works *Dhikri Abu 'Alā* is a critical study of the classical Islamic poet Abul 'Alā Ma'arri (d. 1058). Professor Memon's work on the same poet evoked greater interest in the Arab world and was a tacit endorsement of the contributions of Indian scholars to Arabic literature. The following works are considered standard reference works on Ma`arri: R.A. Nicholson, *Islāmic Poetry and Mysticism* (New Delhi, 1996); A. Nicholson, *A Literary History of the Arabs* (New Delhi, 1996), 313-24.

[31] *Al-Majma`al `Ilmi al-`Arabi.*

[32] Abul Hasan Ali Nadwi, *Purān i-Charāgh*, vol. 2, (Karachi, 1981), 244.

tabligh was initiated as early as 1932. The bond of love and spiritual affinity was further cemented when he married Mawlana Siddiqui's elder daughter, Amat-us-Subuh Sabiha in 1936. Ansari's son, Mustafa Fazil Ansari took over the helms of Aleemiyah Institute after his demise in 1974.

Critique on Orientalism

By the year 1937 Ansari had started learning his fifth language, German (the other four being Urdu, Persian, English and Arabic). Like many intellectuals at AMU, his admiration of Iqbal was on account of his contributions to Islamic philosophy. His poems were soul-stirring; his critique of Western civilisation was rigorous and the message for the Muslim *ummah* was optimistic. Moreover, Iqbal had studied in Cambridge and Germany and his writings were enriched by his stay in Europe. His iconic status for students in India could thus not be ignored in their personal quest to study abroad. Ansari's admiration of Iqbal in this regard was quite understandable. In a letter dated 1937, Ansari sought advice from Iqbal about his intentions to pursue higher Islamic studies in Europe. Iqbal replied:

As far as Islamic studies are concerned, lecturers at the universities of France, Germany, England and Italy conceal their specific agendas under the guise of academic research and objective studies. Under these circumstances and keeping your noble intentions in mind, I state without hesitation that your study in Germany will be futile. Instead, go to Cairo (Egypt) and master the Arabic language. Study the Islamic culture, political history, *tasawwuf, fiqh* and *tafsir* so that you may be able to reach the true spirit of Muhammad (SAW). Again, if you are endowed with exceptional intelligence (and potential) and you are passionately inclined to serve Islam, then you may set out your goals as you deem appropriate.[33]

Iqbal's intuitive insight into the dubious merits of Islamic research in European countries during this crucial period illustrates the negative influence of Orientalism. In fact, Edward Said's *Orientalism*[34] is a critical examination of the growth and development of Orientalism. The intellectual research contributions emerging from Western institution are considered definitive especially in the field of *sirah* (Biography of the Holy Prophet). Their studies are based on concealed motives: to dislodge the faith of Muslims in the Holy Prophet (SAW) from "its firm and entrenched position as the epitome of historic authenticity and moral unassailability."[35] In other words, had the Orientalists succeeded in their nefarious projects of diminishing Muslims' devotion to the Holy Prophet (SAW) then the task of challenging the divine nature of the Qur'an would be a simple one. While acknowledging the positive contributions of several Orientalists for their scholarly passion, their inherited traits of the Crusader mentality towards Islam becomes apparent. Many of the Orientalists have had a theological background and their missionary zeal shows the tendency to present the alleged weaknesses in Islam's primary sources: the Qur'an and sunnah. Again, Orientalism thrived in the nineteenth century in Muslim countries with a history of unchallenged Western dominance.[36] Ansari had an exceptional

---

[33] Iftikhar Hussain Shah, *Tārikh Sāz-'Allāmah Iqbal* (Lahore, 2002), 26.

[34] Edward Said, *Orientalism* (New York, 1979) Chapter 1: *The Scope of Orientalism* provides an objective account about the polemical nature of Orientalism in relation to Muslim countries.

[35] Zafar Ali Qureshi, *Holy Prophet Muhammad and His Western Critics*, vol. 1 (Lahore, 1992), vii – viii.

[36] Said, *Orientalism*, 73. Colonial rule implied a superiority of learning and values of Western civilisation. Therefore, their writings purported to be analytical in content, methodological in approach and reflecting exacting standards of modern scholarship

grasp of the Orientalist project and his writings encapsulate the plethora of the anti-Islam rhetoric that marked the encounter between Islam and the Western world. It would also not be incorrect to state that the garbled version of Orientalism concealed in the hues and forms of Christianity were resurrected in dubious historical circumstances.

Iqbal's advice as mentioned in the letter contributed significantly to Ansari's career. It must be remembered that Iqbal was familiar with the writings of Ansari, which are discussed in Chapter 2.

The extensive reading by Ansari at AMU covered a wide range of subjects. Therefore, it was hardly surprising that he read voraciously during his undergraduate studies. If *The Beacon Light* introduced him as a student of Comparative Religion, his other book *Muhamad, the Glory of the Ages* expressed his mastery over the *sirah* literature and trends in modern scholarship, which were germane to Islamic studies. In this strain, 'Allamah Shibli Nu'mani (d. 1914) provided cogent reasons for writing his multivolume *Sirat al-Nabi*. He says:

> The present day needs of the Muslims have prevented them from acquiring knowledge of Arabic; hence, whenever they feel interested in knowing the events of the life of the Holy Prophet (SAW) of Islam they have to turn to the books written by European authors. In this way the effect of the poisonous information slowly spreads itself, and those affected are not even conscious of it. As a result, a section of the people has come to regard the Holy Prophet (SAW) as a mere reformer who is deemed to have performed his duty as if he has brought about some reforms among the human beings. In their estimation his status as a Prophet is not affected even though he had blemishes in his character.

These were the circumstances which impelled me to

take the decision to write a comprehensive book on the life of the Holy Prophet (SAW).[37]

Nu'mani refers to the biographical writings on the Holy Prophet (SAW) by Orientalists which are based on medieval polemics and hostility against Islam.[38] Even Sayyid Ahmad, author of *Essays on the Life of Muhammad* considered the general pattern of Orientalists' writings on this theme as a 'misrepresentation of plain and simple facts.'[39] Several scholars, like William Muir,[40] for example, had direct access to original source material and it was expected that the principles of a sound enlightened criticism would redeem Western scholarship from its entrenched bias against the personality of the Holy Prophet (SAW). However, their manipulation of spurious reports in early *sirah* literature has largely prejudiced the outcome of their study. As such their intentions are unambiguous: to discredit the noble personality of the Holy Prophet (SAW).

Viewed in this historical context, Ansari's literary contribution on the life of the Holy Prophet (SAW) at a comparatively young age of twenty years must be appreciated. His thorough grasp of the original sources in Arabic and critical assessment of Western scholarship enabled him to present an unembellished account of the Holy Prophet's message to humanity.[41] Ansari's profound study of

---

[37] Shibli Nu'mani, *Sirat-al-Nabi*, vol. 1. English translation by Fazlur Rahman (Karachi, 1970), 5.

[38] Ibid., 98.

[39] Syed Ahmad Khan, *Essays on the Life of Holy Prophet Muhammad* (Delhi, 1981), xix. Cf. Gulfishan Shan, "Sir Syed's Life of the Prophet: Eastern Sources", in Kidwai, *Sir Syed Ahmad Khan: Muslim Renaissance Man of India*, 111-30.

[40] William Muir's *The Life of Mohammed from Original Sources* has been critically reviewed by Muslim scholars. See Jabal Buaben, *Image of the Holy Prophet Muhammad in the West: A Study of Muir, Margoliouth Watt* (Leicester, 1996), 21-48.

[41] Fazlur Rahman Ansari, *Muhammad: The Glory of the Ages* (Karachi, 2017).

the *sirah* is clearly elaborated in *The Qur'ānic Foundations*. His cogent arguments in refuting the Christian-Jewish campaign of vilification and presenting a biographical sketch of the Holy Prophet (SAW) based on Western sources are illuminating. For more than forty years Ansari's writings and lectures focused on the unconditional commitment to the Prophetic message,[42] which is derived from the Qur'an and sunnah. References to the Holy Prophet (SAW) are aimed at establishing a special rapport with his great personality and imbuing a believer with traits embodied in the beautiful conduct of the Holy Prophet (*uswah-al-hasanah*). A detailed examination of Ansari's contribution to the *sirah* genre appears in Chapter 3.

Ansari's Perspectives on Philosophy

As early as 1935 Ansari was invited to participate in conferences in India on philosophy. He delivered a lecture at the Indian Philosophical Congress held at Kolkata in December 1935.[43] The theme was based on eschatological doctrines. Ansari presented his lecture: *Beyond Death: The Islamic Conception of Heaven.*[44] This monograph formed part of the series of *Foundations of Faith*. Ansari's insightful comments about the concept of the transcendental nature and the function of philosophy in relation to religious consciousness are taken from the writings of his teacher, Syed Zafarul Hasan (d. 1949). His book *Realism*[45] a doctoral thesis, is a classic on the subject and was lauded by prominent philosophers and

---

[42] Mohamed, "Muhammad, The Holy Prophet of Allah", in *Islam to the Modern Mind*, 80-96.

[43] Eminent scholars like Mujahid Sharif, editor of the two-volume *A History of Muslim Philosophy* contributed his article on *Dialectic Materialism* in 1936.

[44] Fazlur Rahman Ansari, *Beyond Death* (Karachi, 1996).

[45] Syed Zafarul Hasan, *Realism- An Attempt to Trace its Origin and Development* (London, 1928).

Academic Profile of Fazlur Rahman Ansari

educationists, among whom was his teacher John Alexander Smith (d. 1930)[46] and 'Allamah Iqbal. This slim volume provides a thematic presentation of philosophy, drawing copiously upon the Qur'anic *ryāt* (verses), *ahādith* and supporting evidence from the major writings of Imam Ghazali (d. 1111)[47] and Shah Waliyullah (d. 1762).[48] Like *The Beacon Light* which gave Ansari a first- hand exposure to Comparative Religion, *Beyond Death* represents an important contribution to Islamic philosophy.

The concluding remarks in the monograph are perhaps the first seeds of his dynamic orthodoxy formulation and later developed during his long intellectual career. He says:

> In the end I have to submit that this conception of heaven seems to satisfy all what the heart and the intellect requires of heaven. There is no element in it which conflicts with these yearnings. It satisfies my scientific consciousness because it affirms the existence and validity of law in that life. It satisfies my artistic consciousness because Heaven is a world of Beauty and Grace. It satisfies my moral consciousness because it is the abode where righteousness is combined with happiness and perpetual progress. It satisfies my religious consciousness because it affirms the realisation of the highest yearning of my soul – the vision of and proximity to my Lord.[49]

---

[46] The following extracts are based on the *Foreword* of this book: "The study of the doctrines of modern Realism by Syed Zafarul Hasan is an extensive, patient and sympathetic account of the published doctrines of an interesting group of thinkers of the present day... is equipped for the task and shows a remarkable capacity for appreciating the doctrines..."

[47] Abu Hamid Ghazali, *Kimiyr al-Sa'ādat* (Beirut, 1988).

[48] Shah WaliAllah, *Hujjat Allah al-Bāligha.* Translated by Marcia Hermansen (Islamabad, 2003).

[49] Ansari, *Beyond Death*, 16.

Tabligh Mission in Singapore: 1937-8

Mawlana Siddiqui came to Singapore in 1930 to spread the message of Islam. He laboured intensely in the cause of Islam and delivered numerous lectures in Singapore and attracted many people to Islam. He pioneered the establishment of the *All-Malaya Muslim Missionary Society*[50] which later became known as Jamiyah in 1932. As the representative of Mawlana Siddiqui, Ansari worked tirelessly to promote the interest of the diverse Muslim communities in Singapore. Keeping in mind the hostility displayed by the media which worked in collusion with the Christian missionaries, the task before Ansari was a formidable challenge. This was his first tabligh mission in 1937-8 for which he had to suspend his studies in AMU.

Against the background of the disillusionment which set in among the Muslim communities on account of the domineering presence of the conspiratorial role of the Christian missionaries, Ansari departed from the traditional debate (*munāzarah*) style, and instead, presented an intellectual response to the anti-Islamic tirades. Being familiar with the Western mind which was synonymous with the Crusader mentality, Ansari ably demonstrated the superiority of Islam in the intellectual domain. A detailed discussion appears in Chapter 4.

In a similar vein, the active role of Jamiyyat-ul-Mohammediyyah of Java (Indonesia) in disseminating the teachings of Islam among the backward tribes of Java[51] who assimilated syncretic practices was largely influenced by Ansari. This aspect has not received much attention in the biographical works of Ansari.

In the field of journalism, *Genuine Islam* as the name

---

[50] Information accessed from Jamiat website: www.aleemsiddique.org.sg/index.php.

[51] Ibid., ii.

suggested served as a forum for Ansari to defend Islam against the polemics and often the vilification campaign of Christian missionaries. His series of essays published in the magazine in 1938 acted as a buffer zone against the missionary onslaughts. His essay *Trends in Christianity*[52] was published as a monograph by the All-Malaya Muslim Missionary Society. A number of learned articles by contributors like the noted Indian scholar Sayyid Sulayman Nadwi, Mawlana Abdul Aleem Siddiqui, Justice Mohammed Akbar of Ceylon (Sri Lanka) enhanced the prestige of the magazine. Justice Akbar also wrote an illuminating Foreword to the monograph, *A Shavian and a Theologian,* which was published in 1935. It was illustrative of new trends of Islamic scholarship that was taking place among the `ulama. The typecasting of *madāris* as the sites of conservatism was countered by these `ulama who advocated the fusion of Islamic and secular knowledge. At the same time, pre-modernity cast its wide net on influential Muslim figures and it was not uncommon for the 'ulama to respond to the challenges spawned by these emergent trends. In his correspondence with Sayyid Sulayman Nadwi in 1938, editor of the monthly *Ma`ārif* (Azamgarh), Ansari informed him about his activities in Singapore and his ambition of establishing his tabligh networks in Malaya, China, Java, Sumatra, Philippines, etc. Sayyid Sulayman praised his tabligh efforts and his intention to proceed to Germany to pursue to higher studies. In his estimation, Ansari's doctorate should have positive influence on other Muslim professionals because it was informed by the commitment to serve the cause of Islam.[53] Ansari's versatile contribution to tabligh was widely recognised among the `ulama. Sulayman Nadwi too, was also familiar with the forceful literature by Ansari, in

---

[52] Ansari, *Trends in Christianity* (Singapore, 1938).

[53] Sayyid Sulayman Nadwi: "Shazrat" in *Ma`ārif Monthly* (March, 1938), 162-3.

particular the Arabic review of Ansari's *A New World*. This also meant that this work was being read among the Arabic readership. If *Al-Diyr* promoted his work then the esteemed magazine *Ma'ārif* acquainted readers of his contribution to the steady growth of Islam in the West.

It must be noted that the period under review (1937-8) nurtured Ansari's academic profile: an outstanding scholar with a profound understanding of the challenges facing Muslim communities; an 'alim who framed and developed educational programmes compatible with the aspirations of the Muslims, and a *muballigh* who juxtaposed oratory with pragmatism and Islam's destiny with progressive orthodoxy. In sum, Ansari's intellectual profile symbolised Islam's unique role as a *da'wah*-based *din* capable of responding to modern day challenges.

Academic Honours

In 1939 Ansari was selected as Fellow of the Alexander von Humbold Stiftung of Berlin and was to proceed to Germany to pursue his post-graduate studies. However, with the outbreak of the Second World War in 1939, travel facilities to Germany were equally hazardous and disruptive; thus, he had to abandon his ambitious plans. He resumed his studies in Bachelor of Theology and graduated in 1941 with a First Class First.

Again the period 1941-2 marked a watershed in his intellectual career and pointed out to his remarkable versatility. He took up the MA course in Philosophy and graduated in 1942. His major subjects included Metaphysics, Ethics, Psychology and Islamic Philosophy for which he was required to study the original sources in Arabic and Persian. The pioneering study in Muslim philosophy entitled *History of*

Academic Profile of Fazlur Rahman Ansari

Muslim Philosophy[54] examines the growth and development of this discipline and its close association with the spheres of intellectual thought, sciences, humanities and arts. In this respect, a comprehensive study of philosophy in relation to other disciplines, Western and Islamic was essential. It was at AMU with its distinguished record of producing the best minds in these disciplines that Ansari could not have found a suitable place to pursue his long-cherished ambitions. As the President of the Philosophical Society of AMU,[55] he made important contributions as well. His devotion to learning extended beyond the formal curriculum. On his own he covered an additional MA course in subjects as diverse as Politics, Economics, Law, Comparative Religion and History of Civilisation and Culture. The world-renowned philosopher Syed Zafarul Hasan became the supervisor of his doctorate which he commenced in 1942. Ansari's topic *Islamic Moral and Metaphysical Philosophy* was intended to make groundbreaking research in this field. For five years research work was conducted in an extensive manner. Tragically, in the aftermath of the Partition of India (1947) his manuscript was destroyed during this traumatic period.

His entire library was looted and destroyed in Amritsar (Punjab) and shattered all hopes of retrieving the "fruits of years of laborious and painstaking research."[56]

---

[54] M.M. Sharif (editor), *A History of Muslim Philosophy*, vol. 1 -2 (Karachi, 1990).

[55] Syed Zafarul Hasan delivered an important address to students on the importance philosophy in 1931 under the auspices of the AMU Philosophical Society.

[56] *The Minaret* (1974), 20-22.

Syed Zafarul Hasan: Biographical Sketch

It would be worthwhile to provide a biographical sketch of Syed Zafarul Hasan in order to appreciate his influence on Ansari's intellectual career. Syed Zafarul Hasan was a prominent twentieth century Muslim philosopher. He did his masters at Allahabad University (MA, LL.B) and proceeded abroad for higher studies. He obtained his first doctorate from the university of Erlangen, Germany where he wrote his German language thesis *Monismus Spinozas* in 1922. His doctoral thesis at Oxford University was entitled *Realism* which is considered a classic on the subject. He was the first Asian to obtain a doctorate from Oxford. He returned to India and started teaching at AMU as a Professor of Philosophy in 1924. He also served as chairman of the Department of Philosophy in 1940 and later was Emeritus Professor from 1945-7. In 1939 he submitted 'The Aligarh Scheme' with other scholars, which had political implications in the establishment of Pakistan. In 1947 he migrated to Lahore, Pakistan. After retirement he started work on a book that was published posthumously. Only one volume of *Philosophy: A Critique* could be completed. He died in 19[9. Syed Zafarul Hasan's prolific writing can be gleaned from his attempts to provide an Islamic perspective on Philosophy. His Foreword to major philosophical studies of his students and contemporaries are indicative of his profound learning and immense experience in this field.

The noted commentator (*mufassir*) of the Qur'an and literary critic Abdul Majid Daryabadi (d. 1977) held Syed Zafarul Hasan in high esteem. He mentions two outstanding traits of this contemporary scholar who endeared himself to his colleagues and peers:

- A brilliant scholar in Philosophy he maintained his Islamic identity. In many instances, his outward

Academic Profile of Fazlur Rahman Ansari

> appearance led many to believe that he was an *Imām* of a mosque.

- His lectures in Philosophy bore recognisable traces of an Islamic orientation. Thus, he was able to give a cogent exposition of aspects pertaining to Islam.[57]

In a monograph *Why Religion* Syed Zafarul Hasan outlines the binary opposites of "negation of the aspect of divinity and the affirmation of the aspect of humanity" in order to present the personality of the Holy Prophet (SAW). His logical argument on the necessity of Revelation (*wahy*) through which the multidimensional personality of the Holy Prophet (SAW) is projected is also elaborated in Ansari's *The Qur'ānic Foundations*. Ansari acknowledged his deep debt of gratitude to his teacher (S.Z. Hasan) under whose guidance he learned to understand the problems of Philosophy[58] and through his close association he was able to appreciate the dynamics of Islamic philosophy. Even before the completion of Ansari's doctoral thesis, Syed Zafarul Hasan had recorded his impressions in 1945:

> Rāfidh Fazlur Rahman MA, BTh. has now been known to me intimately for twelve years. He is recognised by his teachers and his fellow students as an exceptional student, head and shoulders above others, always securing a First Class, standing first and often scoring remarkable record marks. For some time he has now been working with me on a philosophico-religious theme for his doctorate, which I am sure is going to be a great dissertation.
>
> Rāfidh Fazlur Rahman is a very capable man and has had a vast experience of the world. Already he has published a

---

[57] Abdul Majid Daryabadi, *Mu'āsirin* (Karachi, n.d.), 200-1.
[58] Ansari, *The Qur'rnic Foundations*, vol.1., xix.

number of books and pamphlets and articles on Islam and Islamic topics which have been greatly appreciated. He is one of the very few really promising young scholars I know of.

In habits and manners Rafidh Fazlur Rahman is a perfect gentleman – who combines in his person true Islamic culture and Islamic learning and I am sure he will, wherever he goes, add lustre to his own self, his teachers and his great alma mater, the Aligarh University.[59]

Sir Ziauddin Ahmad's Assessment of Ansari

Likewise, the brilliant mathematician and Vice Chancellor of AMU, Sir Ziauddin Ahmad shared his sentiments about Ansari's academic proficiency in 1922.

I have great pleasure in testifying to the character and attainments of Rafidh Fazlur Rahman Ansari, MA, BTh (Aligarh). He has been a student of this university for the last many years during which period he has made his mark as a scholar of exceptional talent and ability. He has always secured the first position in his examinations, and has read both intensively and extensively. His knowledge of Arabic and Philosophy - both modern and Islamic - would do credit to any first class student of any modern university.

Besides his brilliant scholastic attainments, Mr. Ansari has also acquired vast experience of the world having travelled widely. He is the author of a large number of publications on Islamic topics[60] and is also a fine speaker. He has now been engaged in research work on an important topic of philosophical and Islamic interest and his work, I am assured, will be a remarkable contribution to philosophical thought. He is equally at home in English, Urdu and Arabic and has an

---

[59] Khalil Ahmad Rana, *Tadhkirah* (Lahore, 1992), 27-8. Cf. *The Minaret*, 1974, 20-1.

[60] Ansari had made his mark with several publications which are examined in subsequent chapters.

Academic Profile of Fazlur Rahman Ansari

excellent command of the three languages.

In a manner and bearing Mr. Ansari is a thorough gentleman, combining Islamic culture with Western learning. In fact, he is one of the best products of this University and he gives great promise of a brilliant career full of service to his nation.[61]

Ansari was held in high esteem by his teachers as well as the senior staff of AMU. His dedication to his studies, brilliant mind and passion to serve the cause of Islam were contributing factors to his literary career. More importantly, this productive phase also introduced him to the rapid changes taking place in Muslim countries, which required the reconfiguration of tabligh for a new constituency.

---

[61] Ibid., 27-8, Cf. *The Minaret*, 1974, 21 22.

CHAPTER 2

Formative Years of Islamic Activism

There are two distinct phases related to Ansari's academic and tabligh profile: AMU and Mawlana Siddiqui. Both were complementary to his vision of Islamic resurgence. In a broader sense, Ansari represented the changing geopolitical developments affecting the Muslim world through his seminal writings.

Keeping in mind the steady growth of Islam in Europe and United States, Ansari's *A New Muslim World in the Making* was a groundbreaking study in the field of tabligh. Written in 1934 while pursuing his studies at AMU, the work may be analysed at three levels. First, the presence of Islam in the West which attracted notable scholars, intellectuals to promoting an intellectual interpretation of Islam. Second, his interlocking activities of tabligh under Mawlana Siddiqui's visionary leadership are articulated. Third, a critical examination of the Qadiani activities, particularly the Woking Mission is brought to the fore. The range and depth of Ansari's familiarity with the trends of Islamic activism are remarkable. Apart from his exemplary academic achievements, his foray into literary writing marked out his fame as a scholar of exceptional merit.

A few preliminary remarks about *A New Muslim World* are important to contextualise its significance. This work was reviewed in the Arabic journal *Al-Diyr* by the noted 'alim and literary critic, Shaykh Mas'ud 'Alam Nadwi.[1] The popularity of the work may be gleaned from the interest taken

---

[1] See Henri Lauziere, *The Making of Salafism: Islamic Reform in the Twentieth Century* (Columbia, 2015). Cf Abul Hasan Ali Nadwi, *Purān i-Charāgh*, vol. 1 (Karachi, 1984), 317-58.

by the Poet of the East, Muhammad Iqbal:

Esteemed and Enlightened Editor:

I came across your review of Syed Fazlur Rahman Ansari's book, *A New World in the Making in Al- Diyā*. But the review did not tell me anything about where the book would be available. If it is not too much trouble, I would be very grateful if you would please send me the copy you have, purchase price included of course, or please ask the relevant bookseller to send me a copy through value post. I hope you will not mind going through this trouble, and to receive my thanks.

Sincerely, Muhammad Iqbal
Mayo Road, Javed Manzil, Lahore (Pakistan)
December 1935[2]

Iqbal was a subscriber to this Arabic magazine, which had been critically acclaimed in the Arab world. In this instance, Nadwah was recognised for its progressive Islamic outlook and unmatched standards of Arabic in the subcontinent. The constructive role of Shibli Nu'mani and Sayyid Sulayman Nadwi in promoting the academic stature of the institution cannot be underestimated. Of particular interest was the popularity of Ansari's works among the enlightened ʿulama who were familiar with the trends of *daʿwah* in the West. Among the avid readers of *Al-Diyr* was the Egyptian reformist, Sayyid Rashid Rida (d. 193X) who produced the widely acclaimed *Tafsir al-Manār*.

Ansari's deep-seated admiration of Iqbal's intellectual writings and poetry, who also guided him in his postgraduate

---

[2] Muhammad Fazlur Rahman Ansari, *A New Muslim World in the Making*. Edited with additional notes by Faisal Ahmad Naqsh (Karachi, 2018), xi.

Formative Years of Islamic Activism

studies, underscored their common interest in the Islamic resurgence project. In 'Iqbal's Idea of a Muslim', Ansari elucidates the poet's elucidation of Islamic renewal in the light of the Qur'an and his unconditional attachment to the sunnah. For Ansari, the 'deadening formalism' had vitiated the dynamic spirit of Islam and shackled the intellectual pursuit that had characterised the Islamic culture and civilisation.[3] This line of thought is a recurrent theme in Ansari's writings and lectures.[4] Additionally, he shared a common vision with Iqbal on the predicament of humanity and the way out as elaborated in the latter's celebrated work, *The Reconstruction of Religious Thought in Islam*.[5]

In his 'reface, Ansari makes reference to the influential figures who contributed immensely to the Islamic intellectual domain. They represented a new generation (*tabaqah*) who worked tirelessly to provide a reformist framework against the backdrop of colonialism. Effectively, colonialism lent weight to Orientalism whose avowed aim was to undermine the primary sources of Islam. Needless to add, there was a surge of scholarly writings by intellectuals like Shibli Nu'mani, Anwar Shah Kashmiri and Jawhar Tantawi who presented in forceful terms the multidimensional character of Islamic thought. Shibli's *Sirat al-Nabi* introduced a new methodology to the critical study of the *sirah* (biography of the Holy Prophet) genre. His multivolume work was a collaborative effort with his student, Sayyid Sulayman Nadwi who rose in eminence on account of his pioneering work in Qur'anic studies and Arabic literature. Shibli's professorship in Aligarh Muslim University also drew him closer to Orientalists like T.

---

[3] See Umair Mahmood Siddiqui, *The Beacon Light* (Karachi, 2016), 343-9.
[4] Fazlur Rahman Ansari, *Moral and Spiritual Transformation in Islam* (*Selected Lectures and Writings*). Edited by Abdul Kader Choughley (Springs, 2019)
[5] Muhammad Fazlur Rahman Ansari, *The Qur'ānic Foundations and Structure of Muslim Society*, vol.1 (Karachi, 2012), xv-xvi.

W. Arnold who acknowledged the latter's erudition in Islamic history. His *The Preaching of Islam*[6] was written in the lifetime of AMU's founder, Sayyid Ahmad Khan (d. 1898). Overall, the nexus between tradition and modernity had a direct bearing on the future of Muslims, particularly in the subcontinent.

Although AMU forged ahead in advancing the cause of educational reform, it made marginal progress on its vision of Islamic modernism. The pervasive presence of illustrious `ulama like Anwar Shah Kashmiri (d. 1933) offered renewed insights into the rational aspects of Islamic intellectual thought. Iqbal was greatly influenced by his grounding in philosophy and progressive interpretation of *fiqh*. He kept regular correspondence with Kashmiri on the advanced Islamic legal thought, which was "illustrative of his humility and keenness for knowledge."[7] In Ansari's estimation, Kashmiri possessed mastery over the hadith literature, ranking him as the greatest hadith scholar of the twentieth century.[8] His other noteworthy contribution was *Khātam al-Nabiyyin* (Finality of Prophethood) - a clear rejoinder to the Qadiani belief. Ansari was much impressed by Kashmiri's tireless efforts to expose the hollow claims of the deviant movement.[9]

The production of tafsir along scientific lines was not a new phenomenon in the early twentieth century. Sayyid Ahmad had articulated the consonance between revelation and nature in his controversial work. The progressive trends in Egypt had already taken shape in the form of *Tafsir al-Manār* by Mufti Muhammad `Abduh (d. 1906). A detailed scientific

---

[6] T. W. Arnold, *The Preaching of Islam: A History of the Propagation of the Muslim Faith* (Lahore, 1979), v. As the subtitle suggests, the missionary activities are covered in greater detail.

[7] Abul Hasan Ali Nadwi, *Glory of Iqbal* (Lucknow, 1973), 18.

[8] Mahdie Kriel, *Islamic Intellectual Revival of the Modern Mind* (Cape Town, 2011).

[9] Ansari, *A New Muslim World*, xx. For a review of Kashmiri's work on the Finality of Prophethood, see Yunoos Osman, *Life and Works of 'Allāmah Anwar Shah Kashmiri* (Durban, 2002), 48-9.

Formative Years of Islamic Activism

tafsir was brought out by 'Allamah Tantawi Jawhari (d. 1940). The noted Egyptian exegete attempted to show the intimate connection between science and the Qur'an through which he brought to the fore the social concerns affecting the Egyptian society. His tafsir had a reformist thrust which evoked different responses from the `ulama.[10] Ansari was familiar with the works of Jawhari and spoke in glowing terms about their importance within the Islamic reformist framework.[11]

Emergence of Islam in the Gest

There are two strands of Islam's footprint in the West. It is a generic term to describe Christian Europe which at the time was the West and subsequently expanded the Western world in terms of religion, culture and attitudes to other nations. In the long history of the encounter between the West and the Muslim nations, it was religion which defined its dominant component. The first strand was represented by the Ottoman Caliphate; its triumphal victory into Constantinople and military successes created a 'hectic, combustible climate of fear.'[12] However, the Caliphate's decline after a series of defeats in 1699 turned the tide against Muslim supremacy in the Christian world. By the nineteenth century Western imperialism came to dominate Muslim countries, directly or indirectly. Even the Safavid and Mughal Empires capitulated to the intrusive presence of the West. The second strand unfolded in the form of the uneasy relations between the West and the Muslim world. A new era unfolded which was marked

---

[10] For a critical examination of the tafsir, see Majid Danesshgar, *Tantāwi Jawhari and the Qur'ān: Tafsir and Social Concerns in the Twentieth Century* (London, 2017).

[11] Ansari, *A New Muslim World*, xxiii.

[12] Zafar Ishaq Ansari and John L. Esposito (editors), *Muslims and the West: Encounter and Dialogue* (Islamabad, 2002), 12.

by the dominance of the technological, military, political and ideological power of the West. A parallel development was the emergence of Communism and its impact on several Muslim countries.[13]

Ansari provides a synoptic overview of the tabligh activities undertaken in the West by prominent Islamic scholars and ʿulama. As early as the nineteenth century a parallel development took place in the heartland of Africa: the clash of Islamic civilisation with the Christian missionary intrusion. The success rate of tabligh in East Africa was phenomenal: Syed Muhsin of Hadramaut (Yemen) converted thousands of Africans over a short period of time, which the Christian missionaries perceived as a potential threat to Christianity. Likewise, Mawlana Siddiqui possessed a charismatic personality: South Africans of European descent entered the fold of Islam. He had been responsible for creating 'an international link of missionary societies' which served as a conduit for the spread of Islam in the continent.[14] Likewise, the tabligh fervour peaked in other countries during his world tabligh travels.

The meticulous details contained in Ansari's survey of Islam's presence in countries like France, Germany, Spain and Scandinavia underscore his brilliant grasp of the dynamics of tabligh. The focus is on the contributions of notable reverts who strengthened the cause of Islam in their respective countries. An interesting point raised by Ansari is their scholarly profile: an intellectual response to meet the religious needs of the growing communities who had been disenchanted with Christianity. Another noteworthy point is the supportive role by influential Muslim figures which included statesmen, political figures and writers. The

---

[13] Ibid, 13.

[14] Ansari, *A New Muslim World*, 13-4.

Ottoman's role (which was in the throes of terminal decline) is a case in point. The growing Turkish diaspora community in Germany necessitated the construction of mosques and other facilities that defined their distinctive Islamic identity. Likewise, French colonialism in North Africa saw the burgeoning presence of Muslims in France who were exposed to a foreign culture shorn of religiosity. Instead, secular values were promoted in line with the integration policy of the state. The challenges were formidable and required constructive efforts for Muslims to preserve their Islamic identity. In a similar vein, `Allamah Iqbal made a strong representation to the Italian foreign minister for the construction of a mosque in Rome, the 'royal seat of Christianity.'[15]

The Muslim missionaries from the Indian subcontinent played a significant role in the dissemination of Islam across Europe. Three names feature prominently: Dr Abdul Jabbar Kheiri, Professor Abdus Sattar Kheiri and Professor Muhammad Wali Khan. The Kheiri brothers, who graduated from AMU, were considered the vanguards of tabligh in Germany and Scandinavia.[16] No different was Muhammad Wali Khan, the 'great silent preacher of Islam' who worked consistently for several years to reach out to non-Muslims in Europe. According to Ansari, he achieved unqualified success in his tabligh endeavours, particularly in Switzerland. The following incident bears out his levels of spirituality:

> Lately the professor was very seriously ill and was under treatment in the sanatorium at Sogano. Within a few days the chief surgeon Dr Graf von Sibberidorf, his intimate friend, Herr Cartier Herbert and the nurse who attended on him saw the light of Islam and became very

---

[15] Ibid., 81.
[16] Ibid., 61.

enthusiastic followers of the faith through his spiritual influence. Among the converts of Wali Khan the name of the learned lady Dora Muller may be mentioned. She was formerly a great enemy of Islam and had used her talents against this faith through press as well as platform. A few days' company with the professor has made her an exemplary Muslimah and she is now carrying on a vigorous Islamic propaganda among her countrymen. It may be remarked about the learned professor that he carries on his work purely on the lines of the old Muslim missionaries and does not beg for funds for his work.[17]

Wali Khan's independent spirit was reminiscent of Mawlana Siddiqui's selfless sacrifice to the cause of Islam is revealing: Mawlana Siddiqui adopted a practical approach to tabligh in view of the geopolitical developments taking place during this crucial period in modern history. The formation of the Muslim identity required visionary leadership that could inspire activism without compromising the Islamic values.

He stood out as an eminent 'alim-sufi who advanced the cause of tabligh as the base for Islamic reform. Like the contemporary scholars he stood firm in his *Back to the Qur'ān, Back to Muhammad* call, which yielded positive results in the far-flung countries during his world tabligh tours.[18]

---

[17] Ibid., 77-8.

[18] Cited in Choughley, *Abdul Aleem Siddiqui and his Mission*, 69.

Formative Years of Islamic Activism

The First American Mission[19]

Alexander Russell Webb (d. 1916) embraced Islam in 1888. He hailed from an equally diverse and cosmopolitan culture being White, American and Muslim. Webb was a journalist, scholar and diplomat whose travels to the East prompted him to study Islam closely. He had abandoned Christianity on account of its complex doctrine of Trinity and the loss of faith soon drew him to explore eastern religions and philosophies. He studied Buddhism due to its simplicity and rationality.

It was Webb's diplomatic posting as a Consular Representative to Manila (Philippines) when he began to explore Islam. It provided him with satisfactory answers on the concept of *tawhid* (Divine unity), *risālah* (prophecy) and *ākhirah* (life after death). He embraced Islam after a prolonged period of study and reflection. Another catalyst for his conversion were the writings of prominent scholars like Syed Ameer Ali (d. 1928) whose celebrated work, *Spirit of Islam*[20] was a must-read in the West. His correspondence with leading Indian merchants and subsequent meetings with several philanthropists in India helped him in the establishment of the American Islamic Propaganda in his country. His tour also included Egypt and Ottoman Turkey where he met state dignitaries and influential religious figures before he returned to America in 1893.

Webb published his first book under the title of *Islam in America*, which was largely a collection of his lectures delivered in India. As the representative of the nascent Muslim community, he delivered two important lectures on the cililisational influence of Islam and the social impact of

---

[19] The term 'Mission' is interchangeably used for tabligh in its broader context by Ansari. It must be remembered that the details provided in the study were, in many instances, an extension of Ansari's tabligh activities.

[20] Syed Ameer Ali, *Spirit of Islam* (Delhi, 1981).

Islam in a contextual setting. Likewise, he published two journals, *The Moslem World* and *Voice of Islam* for the purpose of enlightening the American public about the message and teachings of Islam.[21] By 1896 *The Moslem World* ceased to exist due to financial constraints and the name was taken over by Samuel Zwemer who earned notoriety for his anti- Islam tirades. The initial reaction by the media to Webb's propagation of Islam is satirically described by Ansari: "His (Russell Webb) conversion caused the paragraphic lips of the American press to part in smiles. His return to the US by way of India as a missionary of Islam vanished the smile and produced a guffaw."[22]

According to Muhammad Mojlum Khan, the life and legacy of Webb "remained largely forgotten until quite recently, thanks to the growing American community's desire to rediscover and revive its past. Some have even hailed him as the 'First American Muslim' and books about his life, contribution and achievements are now proliferating..."[23] Ansari's assessment of Russell Webb in 1934 encapsulates the recent studies on this pre-eminent Muslim personality of America.

Islam in Britain: An Overview

The British colonial order had a direct impact on its relations with is colonised nations. Among its major designs was to consolidate 'civilising' missions through the network of academic and missionary institutions. Its influence extended to the study of Islamic culture and civilisation by actively supporting the Orientalist project. At the same time the steady stream of immigrants largely from South Asia prompted a

---

[21] Ansari, *A New Muslim World*, 18-21.

[22] Ibid., 20.

[23] Muhammad Mojlum Khan, *Great Muslims of the West: Makers of Western Islam* (Leicester, 2017), 176.

Formative Years of Islamic Activism

reassessment of policy making with its former colonies. In Britain, Muslim immigration also included the presence of intellectuals who made concerted efforts to create a viable Muslim society. Likewise, the presence of influential Muslim converts added new dimensions to the emerging Muslim community who were rooted on the British soil. In a particular sense, the patterns of change merged with the gradual assimilation of the Muslim diaspora communities.[24] All in all, their collective aspirations were mirrored in their output of Islamic activities and strengthening the cause of tabligh.

During his visits to Britain, Mawlana Siddiqui reinforced the need for Muslim unity which held out promises of the tabligh success among non-Muslims. There were several distinguished English scholars who embraced Islam at the hands of Mawlana Siddiqui as early as 1920s.[25] In the years that followed Ansari would play a significant role in promoting the cause of Islam on an intellectual level. We now refer to some illustrious converts who shaped the Muslim identity in Britain.

Abdullah Quilliam

William Henry Quiliam (d. 1932), better known as Abdullah Quilliam, was born into a middle class English family. His parents were devout Methodists. Quilliam rose in prominence as a successful lawyer. Apart from his legal practice, Quilliam was widely read and well-versed in philosophy, theology, history and science. During this period, he developed a spiritual crisis that led him to the path of agnosticism. The loss of faith in Christianity prompted him to travel to North Africa where he was exposed to the teachings

---

[24] See Humayun Ansari, *The Infidel Within* (London, 2006), 24-51.
[25] Ansari, *A New Muslim World*, 88.

of Islam. After his return to Liverpool in 1887, when he presumably had accepted Islam, his scholarly articles focused on the Islamic culture and civilisation. His rational exposition of Islam is succinctly described in these words:

> Those who cannot understand how 'Islam can be accepted by a European' have no proper comprehension of Western peoples. In the British Isles we are taught to be logical, and to think and reason for ourselves. Islam as a reasonable and logical faith appeals to man's reason, and is therefore likely to be adopted by those who respect and think and have the courage of their conscience.[26]

In subsequent years Quillam's vision of Islam's presence in Liverpool bore tangible results. The establishment of the Liverpool Mosque and Institute (LMI) served as the hub of Muslim activities and within a period of twenty years Quilliam managed to establish the first indigenous community in Britain consisting of hundreds of British converts. As an editor, prolific writer and poet, he published widely and some of his notable publications include *The Faith of Islam* and *The Islamic World*. Through the pages of *The Crescent* Quilliam articulated progressive trends of Islam which, however, did not compromise the teachings of mainstream Islam.[27]

Quilliam was not an 'alim in the formal sense; however, his extensive reading of Islamic sources through English translations, equipped him adequately to be the spokesman for Muslims in Liverpool. In recognition of his contributions and achievements, he was hailed as an 'alim by the prestigious University of Qarawiyyin in Fez, Morocco. In a similar vein, his pro-Ottoman Caliphate support, which brought him in

---

[26] Khan, *Great Muslims of the West*, 189.

[27] Ron Geaves, *Islam in Victorian Britain: The Life and Times of Abdullah Quilliam* (Leicester, 2010), 127.

Formative Years of Islamic Activism

direct conflict with the British foreign policy, was recognised by Sultan Abdul Hamid II who conferred on him the title of 'Shaykh al-Islam'. Officially, Quilliam became a religious authority in his own right.[28] According to Ansari, "Shaykh al-Islam Quilliam made lecture tours in all parts of England and by his profound scholarship effected the rigid antagonism which prevailed in England of those days regarding Islam."[29]

Needless to add, Quilliam was a successful lawyer, charismatic *muballigh* and dedicated Islamic activist who worked tirelessly to raise awareness and understanding of Islam in the backdrop of the deep misgivings by the majority Chris- tians. Many individuals became prominent British or Euro- pean Muslims who in many respects were influenced by the sterling efforts of Quilliam.

Khalid Sheldrake

Like Quilliam, Lord Headley was instrumental in setting up the British Muslim Society in 1914. The key figure, Khalid Sheldrake brought new insights into the activities of the BMS. It attracted a considerable number of converts from the British aristocracy with the objective of providing a progressive understanding of Islam. The social norms of British society were maintained to allow the new Muslims to practise Islam in order to blur out the wide gaps between two different civilisations.

Unlike Quilliam's indigenous organisation, the BMS comprised a sizeable segment of South Asian immigrants. According to Sheldrake, there were prominent figures like Syed Ameer Ali, Muhammad Marmaduke Pickthall and Abdullah Yusuf Ali who delivered a series of lectures for both

---

[28] Ibid., 205-8. Quilliam's pan-Islamic sentiments also was expressed his unconditional loyalty to the Ottoman sultan.

[29] Ansari, *A New Muslim World*, 12.

Muslims and non-Muslims. Sheldrake too, was involved in ''the Muslim societies and clubs that had emerged around the turn of the century. After the First World War, he played a significant role in the Islamic Society."[30] Through the publication of *Islamic Review*, there was a systematic attempt to present Islam to the new Muslim constituency whose intellectual and cultural temperament was rooted in the British soil. Therefore, Islam's appeal to the rising generation of British converts also opened up new vistas of understanding about Islam's culture and civilisation. The rational and spiritual factor that drew them to Islam was, in indirect ways, a rejoinder to the Orientalist bias in the academic circles. The steady growth of the inclusive Muslim communities which spread across London and beyond was a reaffirmation of Islam's strong presence in the most powerful colonial country - Britain.

Lady Evelyn Cobbold

"Lady Evelyn Cobbold (d. 1963) embraced Islam at the hands of an Arab Imam in Egypt and performed *hajj* in 1933 at the age of 66. She has written her very valuable book, *My Pilgrimage to Mecca*."[31] The first British woman to perform *hajj*, Evelyn Cobbold made her mark through her travelogue which detailed her spiritual journey to Islam.

Her first exposure to Islamic culture took place in North Africa, after which her renewed interest spurred her to undertake an extensive study of the essential teachings, guidance and wisdom of Islam. Her expressive description of Islam's positive impact and its remarkable contributions to human civilisation is revealing:

---

[30] Humayun Ansari, *The Infidel Within: Muslims in Britain since 1800*, 131.

[31] Ansari, *A New Muslim World*, 88-9. (Adapted).

Formative Years of Islamic Activism

Nearly 1300 years ago, when Christian Europe was in a state of semi-barbarism, its literature dispersed or lost, the finer arts extinct, Islam arose, binding the wild hordes of Arabia together in the brotherhood of a powerful faith; and in a short time these Arabs produced brilliant centres of advanced Civilization in the chief cities of Asia, Africa, and southern Europe. Baghdad became the home of philosophers, poets and men of letters, and in Cairo, Cordova, and many another city, libraries were collected, school of medicine, mathematics, and natural history flourished, while Europe is indebted to Islam for the preservation of much of the classical literature of the ancient world... To the Arab his religion is a living thing, ever present in his daily life; a power to console in sorrow, a faith enabling him to face trouble with resignation, death without flinching. Truly is Islam a powerful and great force.[32]

Muhammad Marmaduke Pickthall

Muhammad Marmaduke Pickthall (d.1936) was a literary figure who embraced Islam in 1917. His travels to Egypt, Turkey, Lebanon and Syria brought him into contact with Islamic culture and kindled his love for Islam and Muslims. In 1919 he served as the Imam of the Woking mosque, Surrey, UK. The growing and subtle presence of Qadianism in the Sunni-controlled mosque was also reflected in the scholarly journal, *The Islamic Review* edited by Pickthall. His exposure to Muhammad Ali's translation (1917), a professed Ahmadi and other Orientalists' translations, dismayed him. Pickthall's brilliant contributions were visible during his stay in

---

[32] Khan, *Great Muslims of the West*, 207. Cf. Ansari, *The Qur'ānic Foundations*, vol. 1, 219-39.

Hyderabad, a princely state ruled by Nizam Mir Osman Ali Khan. He edited the premier English language journal *Islamic Culture* and also worked as an educationist and mentor. His series of lectures in Madras (Chennai) in 1926 were later published as *The Cultural Side of Islam.* The Nizam of Hyderabad sponsored his venture of the English translation of the Qur'ān which he completed in 1930. In consultation with the `ulama of Al-Azhar university, particularly Shaykh Mustafa Marāghi (d. 1945), Pickthall published his translation in 1930.[33]

Pickthall's personal reflections on the timeless message of the Qur'an are succinctly conveyed:

> No translation gives the least idea of the beauty and fire of inspiration of that book in Arabic, but no translation can conceal from you the fact that it contains a vision and a law for all humanity.[34]

Abdur Raheem Kidwai offers insightful comments on the translation. It is a faithful rendering of the original text. Unlike Yusuf Ali's loose paraphrasing, it avoids the pitfall of a literal translation. As an accomplished literary figure, Pickthall's mastery of the language is imprinted in his elegance of style and diction. Unfortunately, the absence of adequate explanatory notes "fails to advance the understanding of uninitiated readers about the meaning and message of the Qur'ān."[35] At the same time, the notes, albeit brief, do not project dogmatic interpolations, a characteristic feature of the translations of modernist scholars.

The Meaning of the Glorious Qur'ān was widely recognised after its publication. Mawlana Siddiqui who was acclaimed as the

---

[33] M.A. Sherif, *Brave Hearts, Pickthall and Philby: Two English Muslims in a Changing World* (Kuala Lumpur, 2011).

[34] Ibid, 40.

[35] Abdur Raheem Kidwai, *Translating the Untranslatable* (New Delhi, 2011), 12.

Formative Years of Islamic Activism

roving ambassador of Islam promoted the translation among non-Muslim scholars. The following dialogue with the famous British playwright George Bernard Shaw about the Qur'an translation is revealing:

> As far as the translations of the Qur'an are concerned, I would recommend you to read *The Meaning of the Glorious Koran* by Mr. Marmaduke Pickthall, and I am sure that its perusal will enable you to appreciate considerably more the exquisite beauty, the sublime transcendence and the appealing and impressive style of the Qur'an's perspective.
>
> However, I do not imply that it is a perfect version of the original, for you yourself can aptly judge, being an admittedly splendid writer, that, in spite of the translator being the ablest and the best, he can never transmit the force and brilliance of your original writings into his translations.[36]

The translation was written during the tumultuous period of Muslim history when "military disarmament was followed by cultural disarmament - the door of *jihād* was obstructed, so too of *ijtihād*."[37] Like other emerging scholars, Pickthall resisted this trend and made every effort to steer away from the pernicious ideologies on the rise while focusing on the authentic interpretation of Islam.

The Qadiani distortion of the Qur'an, which is discussed elsewhere in the chapter, also manipulated the supposed endorsement of its English translation by notable scholars like Pickthall. Ansari's rebuttal of these misrepresentation is

---

[36] Cited in Abdul Kader Choughley, *Abdul Aleem Siddiqui and His Mission* (Springs, 2013), 141. Cf. Ibrahim Alladin, *Maulana Abdul Aleem Siddiqui: His Life, Thoughts and Message*, 122.

[37] Sherif, *Brave Hearts*, 56.

emblematic of his scholarly acumen.[38] Essentially, *A New Muslim World* is representative of the progressive trends in Islamic studies in the early twentieth century, which encapsulated the robust engagement with Western scholarship amid the sweeping tides of modernism and deviant movements like Qadianism. Before we attempt to examine Ansari's critical examination of Qadianism in the light of its Qur'an translation project, it would be worthwhile to discuss two eminent converts who also made a mark in contemporary Islamic thought.

Julius Germanus

Budapest (Hungary) was the site of Julius (Abdul Karim) Germanus's active literary career in the field of Islamic studies. His unusual interest in Turkish studies led him to study Turkish as well as Arabic and Persian. It was in Bosnia that he gained a deep understanding of Islamic culture. Like many converts, Germanus underwent a spiritual diaspora. Although of Jewish background, he was raised in a secular background as religious education did not appeal to his parents.

Germanus possessed immaculate academic credentials in Islamic studies for which he was offered a post in West Bengal in 1929. The Chair of Islamic Studies was funded by the Nizam of Hyderabad, Mir Osman Ali Khan. His restless spirit and deep reflections on Islam were the inspirational force to accept Islam in 1930. His poignant details of his conversion at Jami'a Musjid in Delhi are illuminating:

---

[38] Ansari, *A New Muslim World*, 90-1. Ansari's familiarity with Pickthall's literary contributions, and in particular *The Islamic Culture* is a conspectus of the former's scholarly erudition.

Formative Years of Islamic Activism

"Ayyuh al-Saadaat al-Kiraam" I started in Arabic – " I came from a distant land to acquire knowledge which I could not gain at home." I expatiated on the decline of present-day Muslims and of the means whereby they could gain ascendancy... Men stood before me and embraced me. Many a poor suffering fellow looked with imploring eyes on me. They asked for my blessing and wanted to kiss my hand. "O God!" I exclaimed, "don't allow innocent souls to lift me above them! I am a worm from among the worms of the earth, a wanderer towards Light, just as powerless as the other miserable creatures."[39]

Ansari has summed up the Islamic activities of Germanus in these words:

In 1932 he made the declaration of his faith in Islam at Delhi mosque and proceeded to his native country where he resumed his former post. But his return to Hungary marks a new epoch in the history of the Balkan Muslims, where the presence of Albania under His Majesty King Ahmad Zugo and some powerful Muslim institution was a sure sign of Muslim revival. In cooperation with Dr Zaki Ali of Vienna (Austria) and Ustadh Abdul Latif, the Grand Mufti of Hungary, Dr Germanus has infused quite a new life into the Muslims of Eastern Europe. At present he is engaged in preparing a translation and commentary of the Holy Qur'ān which is the most popular language with the Muslims of that part of Europe.[40]

Abdul Karim Germanus passed away in 1979.

---

[39] Cited in Khan, *Great Muslims of the West*, 273.
[40] Ansari, *A New Muslim World*, 92-3. The geopolitical developments in the aftermath of the Bosnian genocide (1992) have witnessed the upsurge of Islamic revivalism. See Syed Habibul Haq Nadvi, *Bosnia- Herzegovina: A Muslim State in the Balkan Peninsula* (Durban 1996).

Muhammad Asad

Muhammad Asad (d. 1992), of Jewish origin was a noted Qur'anic scholar of the twentieth century. Asad's transition from Judaism (Leopold Weiss) to Islam marked a turning point in his intellectual life. It was his career as a journalist which took him to Arabia and North Africa. He was impressed by Islam as a natural way of life which led to his conversion. According to Isma'il Nawwab, there were three overarching reasons that represented Asad as a new phenomenon of modern times. First, his belief in the divine origin of the Qur'an and in the prophethood of Muhammad (SAW) and in Islam's message to lead a good life. Second, he was able to demonstrate that Islam's message and teachings are relevant to, and most appropriate for reasonable and thoughtful people in the most advanced areas of the world. Third, Asad like other influential figures embraced Islam while Western powers were exercising their full political and military power in Muslim lands.[41]

Two books written in the 1930s are illustrative of his stature as a profound Islamic thinker and a distinguished scholar: *Islam at the Crossroads* and *Commentary of Sahīh al- Bukhāri.*[42] His autobiographical work bears the imprints of his commitment to the authentic expression of Islam. At a different level, his famed tafsir, *Message of the Qur'ān* shifted his focus to an interpretive reading of the sacred text in a contemporary setting. Like many Islamic scholars who were aligned to the Islamic reformist thought, *Islam at the Crossroad* was a classic work that dispassionately brought out the laws of Western civilisation. At the same time, Muslims were urged to return to the Qur'an and sunnah to reconstruct an ideal society.

---

[41] Muhammad Ikram Chaghatai, *Muhammad Asad: Europe's Gift to Islam*, vol.1 (Lahore, 2006), 137.

[42] Ansari, *A New Muslim World*, 94.

Formative Years of Islamic Activism

Qadianism in Britain: An Assessment

Another centre which claimed to have Islamic legitimacy was the Ahmadiyyah group in London. An offshoot of Qadianism, the Ahmadis have presented bizarre interpretations about the Finality of Prophethood. Mawlana Siddiqui paid a personal visit to the Centre to assess its activities. The Woking Mission, as he observed, did not have a functional mosque with a core Muslim community to express an 'Islam in action'. In fact, there were no markers of Islamic authenticity except a semblance of professed *da'wah* among Muslim converts who formed a threadbare minority in comparison to the established Muslim communities spread across London and other major cities.

The Mission had an 'elitist bias' and made efforts to serve only the interests of this particular 'Muslim' segment, thus deliberately ignoring the challenges posed by the imperialist status quo (British colonialism). Intellectuals like the Ahmadi lawyer, Khwajah Kamaluddin contributed to this distinct Islamic presence in London by engaging in a seemingly academic level on contemporary Islamic issues which were compatible with modernism. In its initial years the Mission strengthened the Qadiani cause in a devious manner. According to Basheer Ahmad Masri, a former Imam of the Mosque, the Qadiani bureaucracy pre-empted the appointment of Sunni Imams in order to promote a heterodox version of Islam. Furthermore, they collaborated with the anti-Islam powers of the day by offering their clandestine services. Their missionary posts in foreign countries had served as a veneer to conceal their collusion with anti-Islamic agencies.[43]

Through its official journal, *The Islamic Review* the Ahmadis

---

[43] B.A. Masri, *The Bane of Mirzaiyat* (Benoni, 1988).

published the literary contributions of widely- acclaimed Islamic scholars in order to vindicate their 'Muslim' identity. Illustrative of their false claims were their propaganda techniques to present a garbled version of Islamic beliefs under the guise of rigorous Islamic scholarship. Their publishing output euphemistically termed 'Free Islamic literature' had sinister designs of luring the unwary public to the folds of Ahmadism. According to Mawlana Siddiqui, the publications were mostly books written by Khawajah Kamaluddin, who was a staunch Ahmadi, while the literature of the Ahmadiyyah Anjuman of Lahore formed its guiding light.[44] The Mission officially promoted Maulvi Muhammad Ali's translation of the Qur'an, which contains a full dose of Ahmadism in a subtle way, and which openly advocates Mirza Ghulam Ahmad as the 'special kind of Prophet', the Promised Messiah and the Mahdi.[45]

A shared characteristic of these movements was their avowed aim to dismantle the Finality of Prophethood creed (*'aqidah*) and impose the divine status of their founder on the masses. Therefore, it was hardly surprising when they developed a parallel system of beliefs and practices to Islam. The element of charisma was employed to bolster their religious profile; new-fangled interpretations were given to the established *'aqa'id* (beliefs) in order to vindicate their dubious interpretations of prophethood. A cursory survey of articles in the journal during its formative period (1913-26) reveals the tempo of their missionary activities at the Woking Mission.[46]

The mass distribution of the Ahmadi translation of the Qur'an was also used by Elijah Muhammad, founder of the *Nation of Islam.* He explicitly cited Muhammad Ali's

---

[44] Siddiqui, *The Ambassador of Peace,* 15.
[45] Ibid.
[46] *The Islamic Review* (Woking), 1913-26.

commentary in his own work to defend his religious legitimacy and to interpret the significance of his mission by adapting terms from various Islamic textual sources. Hence the reference to Ahmadi literature to strengthen his claims is obvious.[47] In sum, Ahmadism loomed large over the horizon and it was due to the relentless efforts of `ulama and scholars like Mawlana Siddiqui, Ansari and Elias Burney[48] who exposed the hollow claims of this misguided sect.

Keeping in mind the spate of Ahmadi literature purportedly claiming to be representative of mainstream Islam, Ansari's critique of this deviant movement has a contextual setting. The Ahmadi branch is synonymous with its literary output, particularly the translation of the Qur'an in English. Mohammad Ali Lahori may be considered as the ideologue of Qadianism for his distortion of the meanings of the sacred text. Ansari has exposed his hollow claims in the backdrop of the movement's insidious propaganda techniques. An understudied aspect of the Ahmadi (read as Qadiani) outreach programme is manipulating the vulnerabilities of European Muslims as well as *muballighs* like the Kheiri brothers. Ansari competently assembled well-documented evidence against the Ahmadi ploys who posed as *Ahl al-Sunnah* Muslims. A collaborative initiative, Ansari quoted extensively from Iqbal's *Islam and Ahmadism* as an academic rejoinder to the Ahmadi propaganda.[49] In the same strain, Mawlana Siddiqui's role in stemming tide of Qadianism in Java (Indonesia) realigned the presence of mainstream Islam in this populous peninsula.[50] Alladin has succinctly described the illustrious contributions

---

[47] Edward Curtis, *Black Muslim Religion in the Nation of Islam: 1960- 1975* (Capel Hill, 2006), 46.

[48] Makki Publications of Durban, South Africa was in the forefront of exposing Qadianism by publishing the valuable work of Elias Burney entitled *Qadiani Movement* (Durban, 1955).

[49] Ansari, *A New Muslim World*, 38 19.

[50] Ibid., 110-11.

against Qadianism in Mauritius:

> In a book entitled *Exposing the Reality of Qadianism*, Mawlana Abdul Aleem explained the differences and controversies surrounding the beliefs and practices of Mirza Sahib (Ghulam Ahmad Qadiani), the spiritual leader of the sect. It was while has travelling on the ship that he wrote this book. He had heard about the practices of Mirza during his visit to Mauritius, and he thought it was an obligation on his part to address some of the misconceptions. He invited Mirza's followers for an open debate to discuss the true practices of Islam. Unfortunately, as he explained in this book, such a meeting never took place. In the book he exposed the shortcomings of Qadianism.[51]

Overall, Ansari's critique of Qadianism in English was a sterling contribution to understand the cross-currents of the deviant movements sweeping the West.

---

[51] Alladin, Maulana Abdul Aleem Siddiqui, 33.

CHAPTER 3

The Holy Prophet and His Mission

Nineteenth century *sirah* works

A critical examination of the *sirah* sources in the nineteenth century may be attributed to the pioneering work of Sayyid Ahmad Khan entitled *Life of Mohammed*.[1] Written in Urdu it has an interesting background that attests to Sayyid Ahmad's deep reverence for the Holy Prophet (SAW). The Orientalist writings of the Holy Prophet (SAW) were steeped in prejudice, textual inaccuracy and misinformation. Among Sayyid Ahmad's contemporaries the work of William Muir stands out clearly for its Islamophobic tendencies.

Al-Khutbat or *Essays on the Life of Mohammed* was written in response to the missionary-Orientalist William Muir's *Life of Mahomet*.[2] One of the compelling motives for Sayyid Ahmad's visit to London was to procure original sources of the *sirah* from the India Office and British Library. Unquestionably, he was fully aware of the need for a scientific approach to present the varied aspects of the *sirah* in the light of modern scholarship. In *his Essays*, twelve in number, the topics raised were addressed to the Western Orientalists and the academic Muslim audience. His analytical appraisal of the *sirah* sources is in keeping with his theological worldview. Nonetheless, *Life*

---

[1] The Urdu version of *Al-Khutbat al-Ahmadya* was translated into English as *Series of Essays on the Life of Mohammed and Subjects subsidiary thereto* (New Delhi, 2002).

[2] William Muir, *Life of Mahomet from Original Sources* (London, 1877). For a critique of his work, see Jabal Muhammad Buaben, *Image of Prophet Muhammad in the West: A Study of Muir, Margoliouth and Watt* (Leicester, 1996), 21-48.

of Mohammed was a significant work that attempted to work out a nexus between classical sources and modern scholarship.

Shibli Nu'mani

A multivolume work, *Sirat al-Nabi* by Shibli Nu`mani and Sayyid Sulayman Nadwi is considered a masterpiece in the *sirah* genre. Nu'mani adopted a critical review of the classical sources to present his comprehensive biographical account of the Holy Prophet (SAW). Likewise, he critically examined Western scholarship which, needless to say, teemed with factual inaccuracies. Their hostility was disguised as scholarly treatment of the hadith and *sirah* sources. A close examination of Nu'mani's discussion of the Orientalists' contributions illustrate the contrasting efforts to offer a sincere portrait or otherwise of the Holy Prophet's noble personality.[3]

Nu'mani was an illustrious scholar whose years of teaching at AMU deepened his expertise in historical criticism and Islamic studies. His fame, however, rested with his celebrated *Sirat al-Nabi*. Ansari consulted this work on two counts: i) it served as a template for *sirah* writing in a contextual setting[4] and ii) it created a robust exchange with Western scholarship in Islamic studies.

Ansari's *Sirah* Contributions: An Assessment

There are three distinct threads that interweave Ansari's multifaceted contributions to the biography of the Holy Prophet (SAW). Unquestionably, *Muhammad, the Glory of the*

---

[3] Shibli Nu'mani, *Sirat al-Nabi*, vol.1. Translated by Fazlur Rahman (Karachi, 1970), 89-96.

[4] Fazlur Rahman Ansari, *Muhammad, the Glory of the Ages* (Karachi, 2017), 53.

Ages is his seminal work. Written in 1933, it is a systematic, well-constructed presentation of the Holy Prophet's life and times. In a series of articles which he contributed to *Genuine Islam* (Singapore) in 1936, Ansari presents a detailed account of *Muhammad: An Ideal Reformer*. Furthermore, he offers a comprehensive insights into the multidimensional character of the Holy Prophet (SAW) in *The Qur'ānic Foundations*. The overlapping features are quite evident in these writings and, in a particular sense, reveal his progressive thought and deep study over the years in this field of study. Moreover, his writings are developed organically which underpins his mastery over the classical sources of *sirah*. Also, he has enriched this tradition with copious reference to the Qur'an. In sum, it is a holistic presentation of the primary sources of Islam.

Muhammad, the Glory of Ages: A Historical Overview

In recent years a few of Ansari's earliest writings have been discovered. The present work, first published in 1936 by Anjuman Himayat Islam (Nairobi, Kenya) had been out of circulation for almost six decades. Thanks to the untiring efforts of Dr Umair Mahmood Siddiqui,[5] he procured a copy from Abdul Wahed Osman Belal,[6] a student of Ansari. Like this work it has been a daunting task to trace other works of Ansari. Fortunately, Siddiqui has competently published some important books which are examined in the volume.

It is interesting to note that the manuscript was completed in 1933. That means that this work preceded *A New Muslim World* which was published in 1934. A revised edition was

---

[5] Umair Mahmood Siddiqui's academic credentials and publishing output are impressive. His *The Beacon Light* and *Fazlur Rahman Ansari: The Ghazali of his Age* are important contributions to the study of Ansari's life and thought.

[6] Ansari, *Muhammad, the Glory*, 16

brought out in 1935. However, there is no evidence of *Muhammad, the Glory* being published much earlier than 1936. An important point emerges: these writings belong to the productive phase of his literary career. Apart from his post-graduate studies and his close association with Mawlana Siddiqui in respect of his tabligh activities, Ansari was a brilliant exponent of the emerging patterns of Islamic scholarship.

Ansari's motivation to write a biography of the Holy Prophet (SAW) is revealing:

There is so much prejudice in the mind of the average Christian that he seldom cares to read a book written by an Eastern Muslim writer in defense of Islam and the Holy Prophet. Our first consideration therefore should be to employ every means which may interest him in the subject. A quotation from a Western authority is often more convincing for him than our research based on original sources. This idea forced me to write this book in which Western authorities have been freely quoted on the subject, especially on controversial points, and though it may not be able to present to the reader all the greatness of the Holy Prophet's personality, yet I am sure, it would be read with greater interest than some of the other books written by the Muslims on the subject and would prepare the non-Muslim reader to proceed further in his study of the subject.[7]

It is a truism that works written by eminent Orientalists are still prescribed in the Islamic studies curriculum.[8] These are unmissable streaks of apologia which have been rehashed by Muslim writers. The lack of originality and creativity are

---

[7] Ibid., 19.

[8] *History of the Arabs* by Philip Hitti is an instance in point.

marked features of their apologetic writings. Curiously enough, the standards of mediocrity are conflated with Western scholarship. Even a celebrated work like *The Spirit of Islam* tended to portray the personality of the Holy Prophet (SAW) with a tinge of apologia. In Syed Ameer Ali's worldview, "Islam is the most liberal and rational religion - the epitome of progress as the modern mind understands it."[9] An updated version of the book appeared in 1922 and was avidly read in the West. In contrast, Ansari maintains that the citation of Western sources is intended to dispel the misperceptions about the 'controversial' issues related to the Holy Prophet's multifaceted personality. These spurious claims are a veneer to malign his sublime character. Muhammad Yahya has correctly observed that the Western subversive designs possess toxic elements to subtly weaken Muslims' faith in the authoritative biographical sources.[10] This work is a bold rejoinder to the web of deceit and manipulation woven by the Orientalist production of biographical literature.

It would be worthwhile to reproduce the following excerpts of the noted scholar Salahuddin Khuda Bakhsh (d.1930), to capture the essence and tenor of Ansari's work:

> It was Muhammad who launched the new faith (Islam) on its worldwide career. It was he who attacked heathenism[11] in its very stronghold, its cherished sanctuary at Makkah, the central point of Arabian idolatry (*shirk*).
>
> Muhammad's simplicity, his humanity, his humility in greatness, his anxious care for animals, his unbending sense

---

[9] See Maryam Jameelah, *Islam and Modernism* (Lahore, 1975), 70.

[10] Abu Abdul Quddus Muhammad Yahya, *Uhd Sāz Shakhsiyyat: Hāidh Dr Muhammad Fazlur Rahman Ansari Al-Qādri* (Karachi, 2018), 192.

[11] Here heathenism refers to *Jāhiliyyah* (Age of Ignorance) which Ansari critiques in his major writings.

Indeed, the mind of the average Christian in the West has become so much poisoned against the great Arabian Prophet that he is not prepared to concede even ordinary virtues to this Ideal Man, and when true things are related before him he either hears them with his mouth and eyes wide open, or, if he has learnt a bit of sophistry, he exclaims at once: "A New Muhammad drawn from a Christian paint box."[16]

The campaign of vilification, according to Ansari, is not limited to the Christian priests of the Middle Ages and Orientalists of the present age, but also to scholars unconnected with the polemics against Islam who have continued to malign the Holy Prophet (SAW).[17] No different was the Christian and Jewish response to the Qur'an. The English translation of the Qur'an by Alexander Ross (1649) is emblematic of the ingrained prejudice displayed by the Christian missionaries and Orientalists. Abdur Raheem Kidwai has ably highlighted the insidious agenda of the Qu'rān translation project in the West:

(Alexander) Ross's work is a telling example of all the characteristics of an Orientalist writing on Islam - sheer hostility and bigotry towards   all things which Muslims regard as sacred; polemical/missionary motive behind the writing; shockingly insufficient knowledge of Islamic texts and serving the sole purpose of misguiding and prejudicing readers against Islam. The narrowness of Ross's stance is betrayed by his labelling Islam as a "Turkish" religion. His audacity in having translated the Qur'an without possessing any knowledge of Arabic is

---

[16] Ibid., 29.

[17] Ansari, *The Qur'ānic Foundations*, vol. 1, 4.

The Holy Prophet and His Mission

Indeed, the mind of the average Christian in the West has become so much poisoned against the great Arabian Prophet that he is not prepared to concede even ordinary virtues to this Ideal Man, and when true things are related before him he either hears them with his mouth and eyes wide open, or, if he has learnt a bit of sophistry, he exclaims at once: "A New Muhammad drawn from a Christian paint box."[16]

The campaign of vilification, according to Ansari, is not limited to the Christian priests of the Middle Ages and Orientalists of the present age, but also to scholars unconnected with the polemics against Islam who have continued to malign the Holy Prophet (SAW).[17] No different was the Christian and Jewish response to the Qur'an. The English translation of the Qur'an by Alexander Ross (1649) is emblematic of the ingrained prejudice displayed by the Christian missionaries and Orientalists. Abdur Raheem Kidwai has ably highlighted the insidious agenda of the Qu'rān translation project in the West:

(Alexander) Ross's work is a telling example of all the characteristics of an Orientalist writing on Islam - sheer hostility and bigotry towards all things which Muslims regard as sacred; polemical/missionary motive behind the writing; shockingly insufficient knowledge of Islamic texts and serving the sole purpose of misguiding and prejudicing readers against Islam. The narrowness of Ross's stance is betrayed by his labelling Islam as a "Turkish" religion. His audacity in having translated the Qur'an without possessing any knowledge of Arabic is

---

[16] Ibid., 29.
[17] Ansari, *The Qur'ānic Foundations*, vol. 1, 4.

outrageous.[18]

Condition of the World before the Advent of the Holy Prophet

The overlapping features in the writings of Ansari underscore the maturity of his line of thought. In fact, the timeline is a clear outline of his intellectual acumen. Over forty years (1933-73) his writings and lectures on the Holy Prophet (SAW) are marked by extensive study, comparative analysis and deep reflection.

Consider the following:

> The sixth century of Christian era which witnessed the appearance of Muhammad was a century of universal religious and moral depravity. The votaries of all the great religions of the world had most ignominiously relapsed into idolatry and immorality. Even the last flames of true religious fervour had been extinguished in the human breast and the civilisation of the world stood on the brink of ruin and destruction.[19]

Ansari portrays a gloomy picture of the *Jāhiliyyah* period which is outlined in greater detail in *Genuine Islam*. The following excerpt is illustrative of his powerful style and mastery over world history:

> At the advent of Muhammad, the great cultures of the world were fast tottering down to oblivion. Every aspect of human life had been sapped by pseudo-religiosity. The divine messages which had come in various countries and

---

[18] Abdur Raheem Kidwai, *Translating the Untranslatable: A Critical Guide to 60 English Translations of the Qur'ān* (New Delhi, 2011), 239. Cf. Ansari, *Muhammad, the Glory*, 36.

[19] Ansari, *Muhammad, the Glory*, 43.

ages had been lost to the world through human interpolation. Theological jugglery was rampant and the followers of different religions, corrupt in opinion and degenerate in practice, were at daggers drawn with each other in the name of religion. The great seats of culture like India, China, Egypt, Greece, Persia and Babylon had become spiritual, intellectual and moral deserts. Arabia, which joined the three continents of Asia, Africa and Europe and was, therefore, the centre of the old world stood as the *centre* of all evils.[20]

According to Ansari, in the fifth and sixth centuries the civilised world stood on the verge of chaos. The old emotional cultures that moulded civilisations and had given man a sense of unity had broken down. In the words of J.H. Denison, "civilisation, like a gigantic tree whose foliage had overarched the world and whose branches had borne the golden fruits of art and science and literature, stood tottering ... rotten to the core."[21] These important observations have been critically examined by Sayyid Abul Hasan Ali Nadwi (d. 1999) in his groundbreaking work, *Rise and Fall of Muslims*.[22] There is a recurrent theme of the *Jāhiliyyah* period to highlight the enduring impact of the Holy Prophet's universal message.

Advent of the Holy Prophet's Call

In keeping with the theme of *Muhammad: An Ideal Reformer*,[23] Ansari gives a conspectus of Islam's revolutionary message.

---

[20] "Muhammad: An Ideal Reformer" in *Genuine Islam*, March 1936, 29.

[21] Ansari, *The Qur'ānic Foundations*, vol.1, 8.

[22] Abul Hasan Ali Nadwi, *Rise and Fall of Muslims: Is Impact on the Muslim World* (Springs, 2020), 1-48.

[23] This theme appears in the articles to which he contributed in *Genuine Islam* magazine in Singapore

Tawhid is the cornerstone that liberated humanity from the bondage of superstition and irrationality. Unlike the parochial claims made by particular religions, Islam obliterated the concept of the 'Chosen People' and restored the concept of human equality and dignity. In this regard, "every child was born pure and that sin was an acquisition and not a heritage." The Holy Prophet's call brought to an end the discrimination against women and introduced a legal charter which protected her rights and restored her divinely-ordained status. Furthermore, social vices were condemned rather than condoned; virtues were promoted to establish a healthy, stable society. By advocating the nexus between worldly pursuits and spirituality, the Holy Prophet (SAW) encouraged the scientific temper which was in consonance with human nature. Ansari lucidly expresses the far-reaching influence of Islam on humanity in these words: "Glorious was the mission of Muhammad, and glorious were his achievements. Humanity will ever remember him as her greatest benefactor."[24]

Ansari eloquently describes the Holy Prophet's achievements framed around the writings of several Orientalists. However, these are not glowing terms as expected but a guarded description of Islam's pervasive and lasting legacy on human civilisation. The nineteenth and twentieth centuries were a turning point in the encounter between Islam and the West. Hardly surprising, therefore, was the armoury of polemical literature against Islam and the Holy Prophet (SAW). It was the calibre of scholars like Ansari who shouldered the responsibility of responding to the slanderous campaigns by employing impressive scholarship. This entailed an extensive study of Western sources dating as far back as the eighteenth century. A critical engagement and scrutiny of these sources were essential to demonstrate the sublime position of the Holy Prophet (SAW) on rational

---

[24] Ansari, *Genuine Islam.* May 1936, 24.

The Holy Prophet and His Mission

grounds. Sentimental attachment apart, Muslims' deep-seated love and reverence for the greatest personality are rooted in the Qur'anic presentation, which according to Ansari, brings out in full the eternal message of Islam.

And We have not sent you but as a mercy for the people. (21:107)

There are two prominent features that make this biographical account an original piece of work. As a student at AMU, Ansari mastered classical works which gave him deep insight into the *sirah* tradition. Likewise, he was familiar with contemporary works by Muslim writers who were not swayed by the modernist tendencies. We may refer to the noted Qur'anic scholar Muhammad Pickthall who is also well known for his series of lectures which he delivered in Madras (India) in 1927.[25] His exposition of Islamic culture reveals his profound understanding of the Holy Prophet's lasting legacy across the race divide. This work also represents the significant contributions by converts who added new meaning to the traditional understanding of the Qur'anic message and teachings. Ansari refers to this work and other articles to counter the entrenched prejudices of the Orientalists. Moreover, *Muhammad The Glory of the Ages* is further developed in *The Qur'ānic Foundations*.

Prophetic Ideal: An Assessment

Several incidents in the multifaceted Prophetic career are highlighted to draw the readers' attention to his humanity. Ansari draws upon the *sirah* sources to illustrate the life-turning lessons that Muslims should assimilate in their lives. The following incident is a poignant description of the

---

[25] Muhammad Marmaduke Pickthall, *Cultural Side of Islam* (Lahore, 1979).

resilience regarding the Holy Prophet's response to the physical and verbal abuse heaped by the Quraysh on his noble personality:

> The Quraysh now renewed the persecution with fresh fury, but the firm stand of Muhammad was a source of constant astonishment to them. They were unable to understand why Muhammad suffered all the troubles so patiently. They thought - and it was in accordance with their own low mentality - that Muhammad desired fame and wealth. So, they sent to him their representative `Utba with grand promises of worldly glory on the condition that he would give up the preaching of Islam and the denunciation of their vain practices.[26]
>
> Notwithstanding their inducements, the Holy Prophet (SAW) recited portions of Surah Al-Fussilat (41) which held him spellbound. He remarked: "O Quraysh! By God, the message of the Prophet is neither poetry nor magic. It is something else. Do not cross his path. If he bends Arabia to his will, you will be greatly honoured; if he fails, Arabia herself will wipe him out."

The *hijrah* (migration) to Madinah was the turning point to Islam's growing fortunes as a cohesive force. The thirteen-year persecution faced by the Holy Prophet (SAW) did not deter him from working relentlessly to advance the cause of Islam. Pickthall has made a noteworthy point about the success enjoyed by the Holy Prophet (SAW) in a land which warmly embraced his call:

> For twelve years the early Muslims suffered frightful persecution at the hands of the idolators, and yet their number steadily increased. The community was scattered,

---

[26] Ansari, *Muhammad, the Glory*, 68-9.

many were driven to exile, yet it went on growing. Though its members were subjected to most cruel tortures, there were few apostates, and many converts to the faith of Allah. Did the personality of Muhammad - the most charming that the world has ever known - count for nothing in that steadfast and enduring growth?[27]

The Divine Revelation (*Wahy*)

According to Ansari, the Qur'ān emerged in history with a distinct philosophy "which in its structure, dimension and outlook differed virtually from the existing religions and philosophies."[28] Therefore, it was not surprising when the Holy Prophet (SAW) claimed that the Qur'an was the greatest of miracles bestowed on him by Allah. Consider, for example, the numerous signs within the sacred text which present the well-established message of universal significance. In fact, there is unimpeachable historical evidence that suggests that the Qur'ān produced a revolution in human history by the message it brought. In Ansari's estimation, the entire system of its philosophy is illustrated in the following verses:

Do you not see how Allah has given the example of a good word? It is like a good tree whose root is firmly fixed, and whose branches reach the sky, ever yielding its fruit in every season with the leave of its Lord. Allah gives examples for mankind that they may remember. (14: 24-5).

Thus, the divine message did not grow through a process of pruning from existing religions but was a 'self- subsisting reality' that changed the beliefs and thoughts of people

---

[27] Ibid., 81.

[28] Ansari, *The Qur'ānic Foundations,* vol. 1, 301.

came into contact with it. Two salient features contributed to the spread of its revolutionary message. The Holy Prophet's entire life was an open book; there were no blemishes on his personality before he received prophethood. He was the embodiment of truth and integrity: the titles of *Al-Sādiq al-Amin* were conferred on him by his people. He possessed outstanding attributes of generosity, forbearance, altruism, etc. that added spiritual grace to his extraordinary personality. His total devotion to Allah is described in these words:

And you (stand) on an exalted standard of character. (68:4)

The revolution which he brought about was rooted in the spirit of sacrifice and *jihād*. It was the Qur'an which guided him in every step of his life; it was its infallible message that detailed the scope and meaning of *hidāyah* (guidance). Brohi elaborates:

Armed by this *hidāyah*, man is capable of being liberated from the narrow precincts in which his reason operates. He is able, thanks to this guidance, to contemplate his total destiny and regulate his individual conduct and the conduct of his fellow beings in the light of the revealed truth which has been brought to him by the Prophets of universal religions.[29]

In the final analysis, *wahy* is synonymous with the Qur'an as exemplified by the Holy Prophet (SAW).

Another important facet that has a direct bearing on the Holy Prophet's universal role is his status as an *ummi* (unlettered). Without delving into the semantics of this word, Ansari makes an insightful comment:

---

[29] Allahbaksh Brohi, *The Qur'ān and its Impact on Human History* (London, 1975), 2.

The Holy Prophet and His Mission

The fact cannot be denied that what could not be achieved up to this day in terms of comprehensive wisdom by the greatest thinkers of the world, and by the greatest religions was achieved through the Qur'an by an illiterate person who had no access to any wisdom of the world.... He gave that Wisdom not through any academic process of research and creation and polishing up thought from inside academies and libraries, but in an extempore manner - orally and in bits, whose collection under his guidance assumed the form of a Book that contains a thoroughly consistent and comprehensive philosophy and code of life.[30]

The Holy Prophet's Contribution to Knowledge

If there was any single individual who would truly be called the moulder of the course of human history it was the Holy Prophet (SAW). His contributions are manifold in the field of knowledge, which may be summarised as follows: he gave man knowledge instead of ignorance, reason replaced custom and tradition, and freedom of thought did away with blind adherence. In a more specific way, the Holy Prophet (SAW) stood at the crossroad of history by "separating non-rational from a rational period of human life."[31] Thus his teachings eliminated the perception that the realms of faith and knowledge are two watertight compartments. Rather his teachings brought man into the world of reason and stimulated his critical faculty.

According to Ansari, the context of the first revelation has universal significance. First, the emphasis of the pursuit of knowledge formed the cornerstone of the Islamic civilisation.

---

[30] Ansari, *The Qur'ānic Foundations*, vol. 1, 302-3. Cf. *Muhammad, the Glory*, 60-2.

[31] Ansari, *Dimensions of Faith* (unpublished), 16.

Second, mention is made of the Lord of the universe Who brought man into existence from the world of non-entity. Third, faith (*imān*) is interlinked with knowledge. In these verses (Surah Al-`Alaq), the psychology for the promotion of knowledge through the pen (*qalam*) is emphasised.[32]

The numerous verses (*ryāt*) of the Qur'an clearly promote the institutionalised pursuit of knowledge. As such there is no room for folklore or hearsay in Islam. In the Qur'anic perspective,[33] the Muslim community is encouraged to unearth all the treasures of knowledge, systematise, classify, refine and promote its cause. The flowering of the Islamic civilisation in which faith and science were beacon lights stood in stark contrast to Europe, which was still in the throes of medieval darkness. Ansari elaborates:

> Those who understood the meaning and mission of Islam projected a challenge to the rest of the world. The world saw a comprehensive revolution by a small group of Muslims, trained and inspired by the Holy Prophet (SAW) and took the challenge to the farthest regions of the world. The Muslims became pioneers on all fronts: they became the teachers in all branches of knowledge and personified the highest moral standards and spiritual values. They were respected for it because they took the lead in spiritualising culture to an extent that many countries became 'Arabicised' like North Africa.[34]

Under the guidance of Mawlana Siddiqui, Ansari was able to expand his intellectual horizon. It is commonly believed that

---

[32] Ibid., 19.

[33] Ansari is emphatic in his assertion that man's role as the *khalifah* (custodian) requires him to subjugate the forces of nature in the service of mankind. See Yasien Mohamed (ed.), *Islam to the Modern Mind*, 120-32.

[34] Ibid., 145.

their relationship was based on tabligh and spirituality. However, this perception has not taken into account the close bond Ansari established with Mawlana Siddiqui while he continued with his studies at AMU. If Ansari was exposed to the whole range of the multidisciplines offered at the prestigious institution to develop his *iqrā* model, it was Mawlana Siddiqui who refined his extensive study of the *sirah*. The erudite *muballigh* influenced him in profound ways that are discernible in his works. It must be borne in mind that that the 1930s were a productive phase for both these scholars in terms of their literary contributions. Although Mawlana Siddiqui did not write prolifically owing to his tabligh preoccupations, nonetheless, his enlightened lectures and articles which have been published as booklets underscore his intellectual erudition.

The confluence of thought between Mawlana Siddiqui and Ansari is brought to the fore in their respective writings on the Islam and knowledge discourse. In his lecture delivered in Tokyo (Japan) before the Oriental Culture Society on the theme: *Cultivation of Science by Muslims*, Mawlana Siddiqui offers nuggets of wisdom minted from his deep study of Islamic civilisation:

> Inspired by the exhortations of their Teacher (Prophet Muhammad), the Muslims focused their attention on the cultivation of philosophy and science. But to talk of learning and wisdom, before a savage and ignorant world and to present a rational religion which cuts at the very root of credulity and superstition was no easy task. Hence if on the one hand the Arabian Prophet had to count with the wild opposition of the savage hordes of Arabia which could be made to subside only after years of wise and patient handling, his followers had also to face similar

situations wherever they went.[35]

The recurrent theme of Islam's scientific temper and intellectual tradition is reiterated in several of Mawlana Siddiqui's writings.[36] Likewise, Ansari brings out the Holy Prophet's contribution to knowledge in these words:

As a teacher of metaphysics and of religion the glorious Prophet of Arabia stands unique. It was he who liberated the human mind from the bondage of superstition. It was he who exposed the falsity of man's notion that the forces of nature were sacred. It was he who, for the first time in history, stressed the great and glorious truth that everything in the universe was created by Allah for the use of man; therefore, he should turn towards nature and discover her hidden treasures... The root of Islamic civilisation lay deep in the religion of Muhammad - in the Qur'an, the glorious Book which Allah gave to the world through the Last Prophet.[37]

In one of his lectures where he addressed the Western audience, Ansari makes pointed reference to the spirit of harmony and balance that the Holy Prophet (SAW) advocated through Islam's integrated approach to knowledge. There was no cleavage between Islam and knowledge, which, in turn, fostered a sense of equilibrium in societal life. Otherwise, there was the potential risk of "sailing in two boats which are heading in opposite directions."[38] According to Ansari, the philosophy of unity (*wahdat*) governs all the fundamental

---

[35] Abdul Aleem Siddiqui, *Dimensions of Islam* (Durban, 2008), 47-8.

[36] Ibid., 10-12.

[37] Ansari, *Genuine Islam* (March, 1936), 31.

[38] Ansari, *Moral and Spiritual Transformation in Islam: Selected Lectures and Writings* (Springs, 2019), 167.

domains of faith and action. Therefore, unity of knowledge opened the way to the conquest of nature through the emphasis of *tawhid*. In the Islamic scheme of things, the scientific quest forms part of *'ibādah*, a revolutionary declaration that changed the course of history. In no uncertain terms, the Qur'an has made clear reference to the unfolding of knowledge for all times as the *i'jāz* ((miraculous dimension) of the sacred text in the following verse:

> *In the time to come We (God) will show them (i.e. human beings) Our Signs in remote regions (of the universe) and in their (own) selves, until it becomes manifest to them that this (i.e. the Qur'ān) is the Truth...* (41: 53).

In the next chapter the shared intellectual affinity between Mawlana Siddiqui and Ansari is discussed.

CHAPTER 4

Trends in Christianity and Communism

Two strands of Ansari's intellectual and tabligh activities are examined in the light of political developments that had a direct bearing on the collective identity of Muslims in particular regions. While colonialism held sway in many Muslim countries, the spectre of Communism loomed large over vast swathes of Muslim territories. It was, therefore, a two-pronged challenge for Ansari to reassert the supremacy of Islam without engaging in polemics, which was not consistent with his academic profile.

Ansari possessed a brilliant mind and this is revealed in his studies. The timeline is important to contextualise his tabligh endeavours and literary output. According to Muhammad Yahya, Ansari had the consummate skills to present academic issues in a charming style. There was no embellishment in his line of thought; rather, it was spontaneous, precise and expressive.[1] His lectures were delivered extempore and held the audience spellbound; his writings were flawless pieces of impressive scholarship covering a terrain of multidisciplinary exposition. Ansari stood head and shoulders above his contemporaries on account of his analytical expertise: any work which he undertook bore unmissable traces of comprehensive study, objectivity and sincerity. He infused new energy into the decorum of academic discussion without taking recourse to sophistry.[2] A young, seasoned writer with an enviable record of merit-worthy contributions, Ansari

---

[1] His lectures in South Africa which he delivered in South Africa in 1970 and 1972 respectively are an instance in point. See Mohamed, *Islam to the Modern Mind*.

[2] Muhammad Yahya, *Uhd Sāz Shaksiyyat*, 132-3.

blazed the trail of journalism. In 1938 he was appointed the editor of *Genuine Islam* (Singapore).

By virtue of his multidimensional personality and active involvement in global Muslim affairs, the spiritual dimension of Ansari's *ummatic* concerns have not received much attention.[3] However, his *Maktubāt* (letters) to his mentor Mawlana Siddiqui bring out the treasure trove of his irrepressible yearning to serve the cause of Islam in the hope of pleasing Allah.[4] Moreover, his indifference to accept lucrative offers and monetary inducements foreshadowed his future career as an outstanding scholar and *muballigh* of renown.

Trends in Christianity: A Historical Overview

Islam in Singapore

Mawlana Siddiqui undertook his first visit to Malaya in 1927 which formerly included Singapore and Malaysia. He began his journey for "unity among his fellow Muslims and global harmony among religions of the world."[5] Singapore, a cosmopolitan country teeming with languages and diversity of cultures, was on the threshold of a new era in terms of its entrepreneurial progress and urban redevelopment. The establishment of the All-Malaya Missionary Society (which later was renamed Jamiyah in 1932)[6] articulated the visionary leadership and the collective will of the Muslim community with different racial and cultural backgrounds. When

---

[3] Ibid., 133-4.

[4] Umair Mahmood Siddiqui, *Maktubrt i-Ansari* (Karachi, 2018).

[5] *Footprints on the Journey of Human Fellowship: The History of Jamiyah* (Singapore, n.d.), 55. The interfaith initiative undertaken by Mawlana Siddiqui resulted in the establishment of the Inter-Religious Organisation in 1949.

[6] Ibid., 57. Cf. *The Muslim Digest* : Jan/Feb 1996, 177.

Mawlana Siddiqui arrived there during this period, Muslim leaders across the spectrum were "attracted by a certain charisma that he had crowded around him and gave him assurance of their support for ideals."[7] He also founded *Real Islam* magazine through which the aspirations of the Muslim community were articulated. Among the pioneers of the Society, Syed Ibrahim Alsagoff,[8] played a prominent role in its establishment. Owing to his untiring efforts, the Society maintained transnational links especially with Saudi Arabia. It was Syed Ibrahim who was instrumental in securing donations from King Faisal of Saudi Arabia towards the construction of the Jamiyah building in 1955.[9]

Challenges in Singapore: Mawlana Ansari's Contributions

It was during the latter part of 1937 when Ansari was deputed on his first tabligh mission by Mawlana Siddiqui. The rise of evangelist activities in the Far East Asia especially in Malaya Peninsula urgently required the presence of a forceful scholar who could address the growing problems among the diverse Muslim communities in this region. In his *Welcome Address* in Singapore he categorically stated that he came as the ambassador of the intellectual empire of Islam to negotiate for reinvigorating and reconstructing the Muslim intellectual life.[10] In other words, Singapore and by extension the Malay peninsula required a renaissance of faith in all aspects of their lives. His pertinent remark about Singapore's future Islamic role vis-à-vis the decline of Muslim countries in other parts of the world reflected his sense of optimism. Ansari was ready to

---

[7] Ibid.

[8] Syed Ibrahim Alsagoff belonged to an aristocratic family (*sharif*) who hailed from Hadramaut (Yemen).

[9] *Footprints ...*, 63.

[10] Foreword by M.A. Alsagoff, in Ansari, *Islam and Christianity in the Modern World*, i-iii.

assist in raising up a great new edifice of Islamic civilisation among people "who entered the flow of Islam at a time when the Islamic world had lost its initial vitality and was on the way to succumb to the cultural onslaught of the anti-Western civilisation and could not therefore enjoy the opportunity of building up enduring and vigorous national Islamic traditions and culture."[11] Therefore, he focused on three areas to consolidate the viable presence of the Muslim community in this region:

- Providing constructive forms in the activities of the All-Malaya Muslim Missionary Society.
- Serving as honorary editor of *Genuine Islam* magazine through which he contributed a number of articles on comparative religion and contemporary issues germane to Muslims in the Malaysian peninsula.
- Organising the Far East Asia missionary front with clearly-defined goals.

In Singapore, the Christian missionary activities gained momentum, resulting in the proliferation of polemical literature. The onslaught against Islam as a universal religion intensified, judging by the spate of literature devoted to its missionary cause. Mawlana Siddiqui's choice of deputing Ansari was indicative of his confidence in the latter's academic expertise. His critical study of comparative religions at AMU prepared him to respond to the vituperative literature of Christian missionaries.

According to Ansari, the logical arguments developed by him in the monograph, *Trends in Christianity*[12] perturbed his

---

[11] Ibid.

[12] A much earlier work, *Christianity at the Crossroads* (Nairobi, n.d) underpins Ansari's familiarity with Christian sources. It was reprinted in *Fifth Pillar*, a magazine brought out by Makki Publications (South Africa).

Trends in Christianity and Communism

Christian friends. They could not possibly challenge his contentions "except that any interpretation on the conclusions of researchers was biased and defective."

Likewise, his refutation of *Muhammedans and Christianity-Twentieth Century* by Archbishop Wand of Brisbane (Australia) was reproduced in the *Straits Times* of Singapore (1938). He argued that the Archbishop's misrepresentations of Islam under the guise of mutual understanding of faiths only polarised Muslim and Christian communities. It was in the spirit of objectivity that the book was written to "clear the position of Islam of the charges levelled against it by the Archbishop and others of his way of thinking."[13]

Likewise, attempts by Muslims to be governed by Muslim Personal Law drew the ire of the media. In 1938 a Bill meant to establish the supremacy of Islamic law in Malaya was introduced in the Federal Status legislature council. The entire press dominated by non-Muslims launched a scathing attack on the Federated Muslim States (FMS) Mohammedan Offences Bill. Among the press the powerful *Straits Times of Singapore* led an editorial campaign captioned "Go to Mosque or Go to Prison" which provoked a series of correspondence and articles undermining the proposed Bill. Ansari wrote a forceful reply in the *Straits Times* to refute the arguments of all the opponents of the Bill. The editor who was instrumental in writing a scathing editorial was deeply impressed by his rational exposition that he wrote another editorial, seemingly an apology and indirectly a tacit acknowledgement of Ansari's academic profile.[14] Thus Ansari in collaboration with Mawlana Siddiqui resisted campaigns which sought to undermine shari`ah provisions in Malaya.

Through the pages of *Ma'ārif* magazine, Muslim readers were apprised of the challenges faced by Muslim communities in

---

[13] Ansari, *Trends in Christianity* (Singapore, 1938), 4-5.
[14] A detailed discussion on the debate appears in *The Minaret*: 1974, 19.

the Malaysian peninsula. On a positive note, transnational scholarship with a tabligh thrust was assuming greater importance and Mawlana Siddiqui together with Ansari were trailblazers in this field.

Islam and Christianity in the Modern World

The hype around *Trends in Christianity* may be gleaned from the barrage of criticism by Christian Orientalists/ missionaries against this groundbreaking work. Employing hyperbolic statements, these scholars attempted to malign the pristine purity of Islam. Their dubious claims of scholarship concealed the deep-seated hostility against Islam and the personality of the Holy Prophet (SAW). In response to these Islamophobic writings, Ansari resolved to cogently address their accusations:

> The accusation necessitated that I should state the argument in detail and prove the soundness of my conclusions by quoting my authorities at length. This I have accomplished in the present book and in doing so I have taken the greatest care that I should select only those authorities who may be acceptable to the Christians themselves. Indeed, a perusal of the book will reveal that an overwhelming majority of the authorities are professed Christians, including a large number of reputed Christian divines.[15]

Scholarly integrity rather than distortion of original sources is the oft-repeated refrain of Ansari's writings. In contrast, the Orientalist writings in general betray their ingrained prejudice to anything Islamic. Archbishop Wand's misleading

---

[15] Fazlur Rahman Ansari, *Islam and Christianity in the Modern World* (Karachi, 2017), v.

Trends in Christianity and Communism

gesture of striking up better relations between Christianity and Islam prompted Ansari to counter these hollow claims. Seemingly, the Archbishop attempted to allay the fears of Christianity regarding Islam's growing influence following the rapid geopolitical developments shaping the new world order. However, his bias against Islam and the Holy Prophet (SAW) is clear:

> The observance of Mohammed's religion was more adapted for the drivers of camels than for the chauffeurs of Ford cars... the doors of Islam are being opened as never before to a sympathetic presentation of the Christian faith.[16]

The stereotypical representation of a backward Islam in comparison to progressive Christianity (read as materialism) is a telling example of the encounter between the two monotheistic faiths. Nowhere is this more pronounced than the spate of Orientalist literature weaving a tale of deceit and sadistic pleasure against Islam. The misrepresentation can be traced back to the Crusader mentality which has not been completely shed by the Christian missionaries.[17] In its resurrected form the battlefield is the print: manipulation of original Islamic sources to portray in the darkest of colours the regressive character of Islam. While highlighting the decline of Christianity in a guarded sense, these writers have not openly acknowledged the pristine teachings of Islam and its openness to scrutiny in any circumstance. In the spirit of objectivity, Ansari quotes contemporary sources as well to buttress his compelling arguments. Therefore, it leaves no doubt that there is no semblance of selectivity (a common trait of Orientalism) to distort the doctrines of Christianity. A

---

[16] Ibid., 2.

[17] See Abdur Raheem Kidwai, *Orientalism in English Literature: Perception of Islam and Muslims* (New Delhi, 2016), 4.

cursory view of the chapter titled *Islam versus Christianity* offers refreshing insights into the accredited Orientalist writers' opinions about the tampered Christianity.[18] The 'Christian testimony' points out to the fallacy of Jesus' supposed new doctrines and the authenticity of the Bible. These conclusions are based on textual criticism, in line with Biblical hermeneutics. As a result, the process of apologetic and exegetic literature gave rise to numerous divisions, further causing a cleavage in the Christian faith.[19]

Context is important to examine the moral decline of Christianity before the advent of Islam. Shaykh Nadwi has succinctly described the chaotic conditions of Christianity in the Roman Empire:

There erupted scholastic controversies about religion itself. These pointless contentions preoccupied people, resulting in the loss of talent and activity. At several places these differences turned violent. Churches, educational institutions and even homes turned into sites of battle. The whole empire was afflicted with civil war. There arose about the proportion of the divine and the human in prophet Jesus' nature. The Melkite Christians of Syria believed that Jesus' nature was an amalgam of the divine and human. However, the Monophysite Christians of Egypt insisted on his divine nature. For them, his humanness was dissolved in the divine like a drop of vinegar in an ocean. The Byzantine rulers and state officials exerted themselves in promoting this doctrine and rendering it as the only creed of the whole empire. Those who dissented were severely persecuted.[20]

---

[18] Ansari, *Islam and Christianity*, 6-29.
[19] Ibid., 18.
[20] Abul Hasan Ali Nadwi, *Rise and Fall of Muslims: Its Impact on the World* (Springs, 2020), 5.

Trends in Christianity and Communism

Muhammad Asad ably shows the Muslim influence on the Renaissance that symbolised the "bitter struggle between the genius of Europe and the spirit of the Church."[21] Ansari echoes a similar view:

> It was Islam, and not Christianity, which brought about the western Renaissance, and the modern scientific culture. The Christian Church, in fact, fought against science and progress for centuries and it was not until it had suffered many defeats in succession and found itself powerless that it signed the truce.[22]

Pagan Foundations of Christianity

In the history of polemics between Islam and Christianity in the Indian subcontinent, the celebrated work. *Izhar al- Haq* (The Truth Revealed) features prominently. There   was the famed Agra debates of 1854 in which Mawlana Rahmat Allah Kayranwi defeated the German missionary, Dr Pfander, by refuting among other issues the doctrine of Trinity and the distortion of the Christian scripture. This work has remained the basis of the Muslim critique on Christianity in India and the wider world.[23]

Islam and Christianity is remarkable for its detailed exposition of the pagan rituals and practices that had crept into the fabric of the once Abrahamic faith. According to Ansari, the pagan festivals, rites and symbols were introduced, assimilated and entrenched as part of Christianity. The disfiguration process was strengthened by a number of

---

[21] Muhammad Asad, *Islam at the Crossroads* (Lahore, 1969), 46. The first edition of the book was brought out in 1934. It was a celebrated work by the former Jewish intellectual, who was considered an influential figure in the reconstruction of Islamic reformist thought.

[22] Ansari, *Islam and Christianity*, 26

[23] See Francis Robinson, Islam, *South Asia and the West* (New Delhi, 2007), 79.

historical factors. Europe was the site of pagan worship before Christianity took roots. Sun worship in all is forms and manifestations was adopted to give it a spiritual content. Likewise, the Easter festival was celebrated in Ireland and Egypt by distributing and eating eggs during the spring season. The imitation of festivals followed by adaptation, which was sanctioned by the Church gave a warped religious symbolism to this pagan festival. This has resonance "in the way Christians do today in commemoration of the resurrection of him whom they believe to have brought a new life to humanity by giving his life."[24] Likewise, the Holy Communion has been borrowed from the ancient sun-worship cults.[25] These rites are representative of the pagan influence percolating the body politic of Christianity.

According to Ansari, several twentieth century Christian writers have offered an apology, in a qualified way, to the perversion that had crept into Christianity. C. H. Robinson admits the debt of pagan thought but regards it as 'a unique merit of Christianity.'[26] For Ansari, many of the conservative thinkers adopt some subterfuge to either extricate or condone these pagan rites in order to give legitimacy to the Christian faith. Overall, it is a futile exercise to defend these rites and symbols against the historical evidence stacked against their irrational arguments. In a similar vein, another group of Christian scholars have adopted the academic path to explicate the theological doctrines in the light of textual criticism. For example, Adolph Harnack, the famous German Biblical scholar interprets the occurrence of miracles in Jesus' mission as the operation of the natural (process) and dismisses the theory that it was an allusion or couched in metaphorical language. This mindset was also discernible in the writings of

---

[24] Ansari, *Islam and Christianity*, 94.
[25] Ibid., 99.
[26] Ibid., 109.

Muslim modernists, particularly in the subcontinent.[27] Overall, these Christian thinkers were faced with the dilemma of lending credence to some of these questionable Christian doctrines; hence, their superficial attempts to create a new conversation on these issues. In contrast, Ansari argues that a recasting of Christianity is not possible for the following reasons. First, if the historical and textual criticism of the Bible is unconditionally accepted, then the flawed interpretations must be summarily rejected. Second, if the Bible is to be believed as the Word of God then its historical authenticity must be unimpeachable and all its teachings must be accepted."[28]

Modernism in Church

Christianity underwent dramatic changes, particularly in the fifteenth century when it split into two major sects: Catholicism and Protestantism. The latter was a reaction to the rigid doctrines adopted by the Church of Rome and developed into a distinct sect with a set of beliefs and practices. The Reformation initiated by Martin Luther (d. 1546) ultimately led to the schism of the Church.

By the nineteenth century, there were intense debates within the Protestant Church regarding cardinal issues that formed the core beliefs of this sect. According to Ansari, the modernists challenged the authenticity of the Bible, by declaring the incompetence of the priests (clergy). They also cast doubts about the divinity of Jesus which they argued had no connection with his virgin-birth. Additionally, the stories relating to the creation of women and the Daniel accounts had toxic elements of incredulity. In other words, these stories

---

[27] Sayyid Ahmad Khan, founder of Aligarh Muslim University is a case in point.
[28] Ibid., 141.

which were taught for instructive purpose undermined the rational aspect of religious truth.

Keeping in mind the science and religion debate, the modernists were critical of the theologians who condemned the scientific findings by distinguished thinkers and scientists. Copernicus (d. 1543) was a famed mathematician and astronomer who proposed that the sun was stationary in the centre of the universe. This theory was condemned by the theologians who gave bizarre explanations about the cosmos. Not surprisingly, therefore, were the modernists' strong objections to the irrational beliefs of the Church on doctrinal issues. Notwithstanding the progressive thought advanced by the modernists, Ansari forcefully presses home an important point: Reformed Christianity will not make any significant strides if it is devoid of divine revelation (*wahy*). "It is in Islam and Islam alone that a Christian should seek to get the required transformed Christianity" as has been lucidly expressed in the Qur'ān.[29]

Islam as the Future Religion

Ansari is among the pioneering scholars who had documented the growth of Islam in the West. The statistics of influential figures who accepted Islam alarmed the missionaries. The notorious missionary, Samuel Zwemer was constrained to acknowledge the growing presence of Islam in the West:

The old missionary slogan has met with a counter slogan. Islam is challenging the West to accept Mohammed as the hope of humanity... Mohammed has discovered America... In North America there are scattered groups numbering, it is true, twelve thousand only but

---

[29] Ibid., 152.

Trends in Christianity and Communism

active in their propaganda... The conversion of Europeans and Americans has become a stock-in-trade argument against Christianity in Egypt and India.[30]

Mojlum Khan's comprehensive work on Muslim converts also covers influential figures of the twentieth century. Apart from some notable mentions in Chapter 2, two converts from England are discussed by Ansari and Khan. Lord Henry Stanley of Alderly (d.1925) was the British ambassador to Turkey and a member of the British parliament. According to Khan, he was in many ways a model British Muslim who left a remarkable legacy which could foster a uniquely British Muslim identity.[31] Likewise, John Yahya Parkinson (d. 1918) made a critical study of Christianity and found its theology unimpressive and over time led him to Islam. His series of articles were published in the *Islamic Review* and was lauded in academia. Parkinson was a gifted scholar and thinker "who was equally steeped in Western intellectual thought, in addition to being an assiduous critic of Christian theology and history." In other words, he pursued a more systematic and scholarly approach to aspects of Islamic thought, Western philosophy and Christology than any of his contemporaries..."[32] Keeping in mind that *Islam and Christianity* was published in 1940, Ansari's systematic study of Islam in the West is impressive.

In the final analysis, Ansari addresses the Christian world in these words:

[The study] is meant to bring out the fundamental distinction of Islam from non-Islam, and to show that the notion of religion in Islam is infinitely richer and more sound than any other to which humanity subscribes. I am confident that those of my Christian readers who

---

[30] Cited in Ansari, *Islam and Christianity*, 184-5.
[31] Mojlum Khan, *Great Muslims of the West*, 167.
[32] Ibid., 237.

undertake an impartial and detailed study of Islam will come to the same conclusion and join me in saying: "God's choicest blessings be on His beloved Prophet Muhammad for the light and guidance he brought to humanity!"[33]

On a positive note, Ansari reminds sincere Christians that Islam does not subscribe to the notion that the universe is composed of two conflicting entities. It conceives life as a unity reflecting divine oneness and gives clear meaning to the purpose of life, whether it is physical or spiritual. In Islam, harmony proceeds from the sense of equilibrium which allows man to realise his full potential as Allah's *khalifah* (custodian) on earth. Ansari explains:

Thus, our earthly surroundings are not a meaningless projection of the play of blind forces - a mere empty shell with no content. Nay, the tiniest particle of sand, the smallest drop of water, the frailest rose-leaf is full of meaning and music and functions under a definite and well-planned Divine scheme.[34]

In the spirit of scholarly rapprochement Ansari makes a candid observation:

Will Islam succeed where Christianity has failed? For instance, Lord Lothian, the well-known British statesman, in his Convocation Address to the students of AMU, said: "The day of purely personal religion, or the kind of religion which comforts and sustains the individual... and partly by promising salvation, that day I believe, has passed away. The modern scientific man brings everything, even Truth itself, to the proof of results. If he

---

[33] Ansari, *Islam and Christianity*, 212-3.
[34] Ibid., 201.

is to follow religion, he demands that religion should show him how to set about solving the practical problems of man, and not merely promise him Nirvana after an immense series of re-births, or a heaven whose nature is indeterminate and which can only be reached through the portal of death. Religion must not only give him the key to the riddle of the universe; it must show him with scientific accuracy and results, how to control the new forces which threaten to destroy rather than to benefit mankind."[35]

The spectre of Communism foreshadowed the brutality of an ideological system hellbent on destroying humanity.

Communist Challenge to Islam

The noted Pakistani scholar, Umair Mahmood Siddiqui has provided a brief overview of Ansari's critique on Communism. The book[36] was published in 1951 under the auspices of Makki Publications (Durban, India). Ansari had by the left his left position as an officer-in-charge of the Sindh government weekly journal, *Sindh Information*. The position stiled his creative abilities to serve the cause of Islam. The first publisher of the book, Mohammed Makki spoke in glowing terms about its content: "[It] is a successful attempt to throw up in bold relief the significance of Communism to the Islamic world. Here is an analysis and commentary, substantiated by documentary evidence which gives a convincing account of what Communism means to good Muslims."[37]

The Preface of this merit-worthy book outlines Ansari's motivation to undertake a comprehensive study of

---

[35] Ibid., 191-2.

[36] Muhammad Fazlur Rahman Ansari, *Communist Challenge to Islam: An Exposition of Communism vis-à-vis Islam* (Karachi, 2018). The present work includes *Islam versus Marxism* and *Islam versus Communism*.

[37] Ibid., 16-7.

Communism. The Communist propaganda had caught the imagination of the 'half-religious nationalist' and the naïve religious-minded Muslims who believed that this ideology was close in spirit to the egalitarian views of Islam. Ansari countered these misperceptions by exposing the sinister ploys of this ideology so that Muslims may be wary of its pretentious sympathy to Islam. The timeline of this work clearly suggests that it was commenced in Aligarh. There were several articles which were written for reputed magazines on the Communist threat to Islam. In fact, the Islamic Research Academy was inaugurated in 1943 at AMU under the patronage of Mawlana Siddiqui.[38] Ansari's doctoral supervisor, Syed Zafarul Hasan[39] also made noteworthy contributions to the Academy.

Communism: A Critique

Before we attempt to critically examine the nature of Communism, it will be useful to locate the principle of *tawhid* in man's life. According to Ismail Faruqi, "*tawhid* is a general view of reality, of truth, of the world, of space and time, of human history and destiny."[40] In other words, *tawhid* is the essence of Islam from which flows the central idea of total obedience to Allah, His commandments as expressed in the Qur'an and exemplified in the sunnah. The completeness of Islam is synonymous with the principle of *tawhid*; therefore, no ideology can influence or adapt Islam, which is a *din* (complete code of life).

Without delving into the history of Communism which was preceded by Marxism, these two ideological systems argued

---

[38] Ibid., 38-9.

[39] Ansari's doctoral thesis entitled *The Islamic Moral and Metaphysical Philosophy*.

[40] Ismail Raji Faruqi, *Al-Tawhid: Its Implication for Thought and Life* (Herndon, 1992), 10.

Trends in Christianity and Communism

that religion was the 'opium of the people' and the plight of man rest in their blind acceptance of capitalism.

However, Communism implemented a superficial classless society by negating economic opportunities and stifling freedom of expression and movement of the masses. Worse was its oppressive policies that oversaw the genocide of millions of innocent people. The iron mould of the Conmmunist dictatorship under Stalin was also cast in merciless exploitation and degradation of Muslims in Central Asia. Ansari has painted a grim picture of the persecution of Muslims in this region, who represented the pride of Muslim culture and civilisation. Effectively, the fall of the state of Bukhara made the Communists "the de facto rulers of the whole of Muslim Central Asia."[41] The consequences were grave: mosques and *maktabs* were shut down, the 'ulama were persecuted, the Qur'an was banned and any vestige of Islamic identity was eradicated. These harsh measures forced the *sui* orders to continue with their activities clandestinely.[42] An alarming development was the abolition of the Arabic script, very much reminiscent of Kemal Ataturk's de-Islamisation policy. The change of the alphabet alone "was enough to bring about a revolution in the life of the Turkish nation by giving birth to a new and rootless generation, ignorant of its cultural inheritance."[43] Ansari's terse comments are illustrative:

The third step was to replace the Arabic alphabet by Latin alphabet and thus to cut off the Muslims from the rest of the world, on the one hand, and form their whole Islamic religious and cultural past, on the other. Thenceforth, Islamic tradition as enshrined in their national literature

---

[41] Ansari, *Communist Challenge to Islam*, 181.

[42] Ibid., 210-3.

[43] Abul Hasan Ali Nadwi, *Western Civilisation, Islam and Muslims* (Lucknow, 1974), 57.

was to be a sealed book for the coming generations.[44]

Ansari's timeline approach to Communism reveals his remarkable depth of knowledge and mastery over the primary sources. Of particular interest is the indoctrination process among the youth. For historical reasons, disillusionment set in among these disaffected Muslim youth who embraced the Communist ideology. Obviously, the aggressive propaganda and ideological ploys were optimally used to tarnish the image of Islam as a religion of 'backwardness and retrogression'. Young Muslim women were the primary target of the Communist 'progressive' policies and were led to believe that the veil (*paranja*) was an impediment to their emancipation from the male-dominated society.[45] The feminist voice was amplified to denigrate the status of women in Islam. Likewise, revolutionary works by Muslim intellectuals were promoted as deceptive tools of modernity, which were aimed to give a sanitised version of Communism. Amid these anti-Islamic slogans was the intrusion of materialism.[46] Tragically, the moral code of Islam was discarded for a utopian ideal: economic prosperity unfettered by religion.

Ansari countered the Communist policy of disinformation as a propaganda tool for disseminating its sympathetic views on Islam. Furthermore, the ruthless subjugation of Muslim states, *khanates* which were autonomous for centuries, was a tell-tale sign of Islam's waning presence. Ansari says:

> The concessions were made. The anti-religious policy was relaxed. But the purpose was not to resuscitate the religious life. Therefore, the moment the Communist leaders discerned signs of a sort of religious revival among the Muslims, warnings immediately went forth from the

---

44 Ansari, *Communist Challenge to Islam*, 201-2.
45 Ibid., 204-5.
46 Ibid., 214-6.

masters to the slaves to remain 'within limits'. After the war was over, these warnings became more and more pronounced.[47]

Islam and Communism

Ansari's incisive analysis of Communism is illustrative of his thorough grounding in philosophy and politics. Avoiding the anti-religion (atheism) rhetoric, very much evident in the writings of Muslim scholars in general, Ansari undertook a systematic study of this ideological system by highlighting its flawed worldview. At the same time, he critically examined Capitalism for its materialistic conception of life. Both these ideologies veered in opposite directions. According to Ansari, the Muslim community follows the path of *wasatiyyah*[48] - the middle of the road - in the elimination of the evils of poverty, on the one hand, and the evils of riches, on the other.

Islam steers the middle course between Capitalism and Communism and bears witness to the evil of their extremism - an evil from which they them- selves are trying to recede gradually, thus proving the truth of Islam. The famous philosopher of histo- ry, Professor Arnold Toynbee admits: " If Russia has moved to 'the right' her neighbours have moved to 'the left'... the apparently irresistible encroachment of planning on the once unregimented economies of the democratic countries suggest that the social structure of all countries in the near future is like to be both national and socialist. Not only do the Capitalist and Communist regimes seem likely to

---

[47] Ibid., 220.

[48] *Thus We have appointed you (O Muslims) a middle nation (or, a nation conforming to the just mean), that you may be witnesses against mankind, and that the Messenger (Muhammad) may be in regard to you a witness...* (2: 143).

continue side by side; it may well be that Capitalism and Communism are becoming different names for very much the same things."[49]

As explained in the chapter, *Communist Challenge to Islam* was written at a critical period in the twentieth century when Muslims' surrender to the Communism was a grim reality. The rise of despotic Muslim regimes posed an existential threat to Muslim organisations advancing the cause of an Islamic state. Egypt was representative of this trend. The ruthless attempt to put an end to the Ikhwan movement under the charismatic leadership of Hasan Al- Banna (d.1949) also paved the way for the encroachment of Communism in the country. In the same strain, Ansari warned against the forces of conservatism which had struck deep roots in the Muslim mindset and failed to stem the tide of atheism on rational grounds.[50] Pan-Islam or progressive orthodoxy, as Ansari coined the term, was able to infuse into the *ummah* renewed levels of faith against the growing presence of Socialism advocated by President Nasser.[51]

Communism: A Synoptic Assessment

Under the mentorship of Mawlana Siddiqui, Ansari wrote a series of monographs on the Communism theme. Mawlana Siddiqui's tabligh travels which included regions like the present Xinjiang province in China, exposed him to the nefarious designs of Communism. His familiarity with the

---

[49] Ansari, *The Qur'ānic Foundations*, vol.2, 421.

[50] Ansari, *Communist Challenge to Islam*, 56-7.

[51] Nadwi, *Western Civilisation, Islam and Muslims*, 112. The Egyptian Revolution of 1952 was conceived on the foundations of Communism and materialistic nationalism, which would transform the Egyptian and Arab society. Ansari's comments have relevance in the context of the prevailing circumstances in Egypt.

Trends in Christianity and Communism

Marxist and Communist discourse is ably brought out in his book *How to Face Communism*. According to Mawlana Siddiqui, the prevalent ideological systems posed a powerful challenge to tabligh. In this respect, his critique of Communism (interchangeably used for Marxism) identified its distinguishing features which had shackled millions of souls in total subservience to its ruthless policies. He observed:

It is said that the evils of capitalism have compelled the starting millions to rise in revolt; that the exploitation of the power by the rich have forced them into convict and that the only way in which to establish justice is nothing but war. There is no doubt that the exploitation and oppression of mankind should be stopped and the destiny and prosperity of the common man should be secured. We have to be on guard against those who are out to use this struggle for social justice for gaining certain ulterior ends of their own. The Marxists or the Communists for instance are employing the poverty line in certain countries as an instrument of their aggression. They appeal to the people in the name of human equality and ask them to wage class warfare, but the theory as well as the actions of the Marxists and the Communists is a positive proof that the success of Marxism puts the people into evils even worse than those which it aims to fight.

The success of Marxism means the way to atheism and the mechanical acceptance of certain creeds which are after all man-made. Marxism further means wide suppression of the faith in God. Who has not heard the words of Karl Marx that belief in God is a fraud and that religion is the opium for the people. Marxism cannot tolerate the faith, the brotherhood and the unity of mankind which is based on the faith in the one Supreme Being, the true God. Anyone who has studied the books of Marx will completely agree with me.[52]

Mawlana Siddiqui expended his energies to counteract the menace of Communism during his tabligh travels. Books written under his guidance especially by Ansari[53] were intended to raise a global awareness of the tragic consequences created by these ideological systems. The fate of Turko-Tartars was a microcosm of the large chunks of Muslim nations suffering miserably under the Communist regime.

The collaborative efforts by Mawlana Siddiqui and Ansari to raise awareness of the Communist threat on an academic level point out to their proactive role as bastions of Islamic *'ulum*. They broadened the scope of tabligh, which was restricted to preaching and teaching. For these erudite scholars, several Muslim countries were on the cusp of achieving their respective independence from colonial rule. However, their leadership continued to serve the vested interests of their colonial masters and made concerted efforts to stamp out any vestige of the shari'ah. Modernism, for example, made its imprints in the former French colonies. New models of government bore no affinity to the religious and cultural aspirations of Muslim nations. More alarming was the intrusive presence and aggressive policies of Communism to dislodge the collective Islamic identity of the populous Muslim regions. Moreover, the rivalry between the Capitalist Economy and Communist hegemony had severe repercussions across the world. It is in this context that two important works of Ansari are contextualised in specific

---

[52] Abdul Aleem Siddiqui, *How to Face Communism* (Karachi, n.d.), 15-6. Cf. Alladin, *Maulana Abdul Aleem Siddiqui*, 131. The amalgam of moral and spiritual values in Islam is emphasised.

[53] The following books written by Ansari were intended to refute Communist doctrines:

- *Islam versus Communism* (Karachi, 1982).
- *Islam versus Marxism* (Karachi, 1982).

Trends in Christianity and Communism

settings. They represent the maturity of his intellectual thought and deep reflections on these ideological systems.

Islam versus Marxism was an essay written for the Muslim-Christian Convention held in Beirut, London in 1954. Four themes were explored by Ansari: the spiritual assets in Islam, concept of social work in Islam, the social challenge to Islam and reaching out to the youth based on Islam's spiritual values.[54]

Ansari proposed the following measures to stem the tide of Marxism:

Practically speaking, there can be only two mediums for the transmission (of Islamic values) besides the home, pulpit and press: namely, the state and educational institutions. Therefore, the entire system of popular education prevalent in the Muslim countries should be reformed and reconstituted in such a way as to make every institution a vehicle for the transmission of the theoretical and practical aspects of the Islamic philosophy of life. The Muslim state should reform itself and its constitution in such a manner as to become capable of fulfilling all the obligations ... of establishing the practical model of Islamic political, economic and social teachings.[55]

As an international *muballigh* and distinguished scholar, Ansari was invited to South Africa in 1970 to deliver a series of talks. His lectures on *Islam and Marxism* and *Islam versus Communism*[56] contained a thematic message: ideologies are antithetical to the spirit of Islam. It must be remembered that Ansari's lectures were extempore and he was an ocean of knowledge (*bahr-al 'ulum*) in his critical examination of ideologies like Marxism and Communism.

---

[54] Ansari, *Communist Challenge to Islam*, 230.
[55] Ibid., 248.
[56] Mohamed, *Islam to the Modern Mind*, 204-10.

What set Ansari apart from academics and `ulama was his proficiency in Islamic and secular disciplines. According to Ansari, Marxism and Communism thrived on the notion of materialism and expediency.[57] If Marxism opposed capitalism it promoted materialism as an alternative which operated in a godless culture. Likewise, Communism believed in the participation of the proletariat: a deceptive tool to entrench the dictatorship by a select few.[58] Islam condemned these ideological systems because they deprived mankind of their intrinsic values and highest yearnings, including the moral and spiritual system. Again, the theme of *khilāfah,* man's divine responsibility is emphasised.

Ansari's critique of Marxism and Communism must be seen in relation to Muslim leaders who established political alliance with Communist countries in the early 1970s.[59] The consequences were disastrous for both Islam and the *ummah.* Muslim leadership was a hybrid of de-Islamised and de-culturised elements with no faith in the dynamic spirit of Islam. Likewise, Ansari expressed his candour at Muslims' impotence to resist the challenges of materialism advanced by Marxism. In his insightful lecture, *Materialism: A Challenge to World Religions*[60] Ansari reiterated Muslim predicament in the country (South Africa) within the context of sociopolitical challenges. He said that Muslims needed a definite, positive and dynamic effort to go back to Allah, back to the higher values as exemplified by the holy personalities whom Allah had sent to various communities of mankind. In his estimation, equality of mankind was synonymous with the honour Allah had conferred on the children of Adam. This

---

[57] Ibid., 208.

[58] Ibid.

[59] Pakistan's alliance with Russia which also veered towards India for political expediency is one example. See, Zafique Ahmad, *Pakistan India Relations* (Lahore, 1989).

[60] Mohamed, *Islam to the Modern Mind,* 288-94.

Trends in Christianity and Communism

implied that Muslims should re- assess their role in life. A bold step, Ansari contended, was to understand the implication of the call to "Discover God again." It involved "a real vibrant, dynamic and living faith in Him.'[61] A community inspired by goals reflecting the Islamic principles of goodwill, and selfless love for mankind can confront the 'hydra-headed monster of materialism and permissive society.'"[62]

In sum, Communism was not an independent ideology that changed the course of world events. Rather, it was nurtured on the soil of secularism and materialism, offshoots of Western civilisation. According to Ansari, Communism operated as a dysfunctional system hindering the complete development of the human personality. As a result, "it gave the world for the first time in human history the most thorough and most aggressive materialistic philosophy."[63]

---

[61] Ibid., 291.
[62] Ibid., 291-2.
[63] Ansari, *Islam and Western Civilisation* (Karachi, 1983), 4.

CHAPTER 5

Perspectives on the Islamisation of Knowledge

In Chapter 1, a synoptic overview of the *Dars i-Nizāmi* was given. There is a general perception among modernist Muslims that the curriculum was outdated and largely responsible for the intellectual decline in the Indian subcontinent. For historical reasons this mindset has taken roots in the present century with the result that conservatism is associated with the *Dars i-Nizāmi*. The stereotyping of the existing system of Islamic education has stymied the scholarly examination of its evolution and geographical spread in the subcontinent and beyond.

In the mid-twentieth century, a prominent scholar, Mawlana Manazir Ahsan Gilani, proposed reforms to the madrasah curriculum. He recommended that the *Dars i-Nizāmi* required "a certain intellectual maturity to fully understand its purposes and goals. This can only be fruitfully mined at a graduate level, where it will deliver optimal dividends."[1] A revised curriculum in keeping with the challenges of the modern age was also deliberated among the `ulama. Notwithstanding these enlightened opinions, the pace of reform was negligible. Another serious deficiency in the system was in the area of specialisation.[2] In the heyday of Islamic civilisation the curriculum had a specialist edge and produced scholars of eminence. This synergy was embodied in the *iqrā* paradigm and was a trailblazer in the field of education.

Two factors account for Ansari's scholarly presentation of

---

[1] Ebrahim Moosa, *What is a Madrasa* (Chapel Hill, 2015), 138.
[2] Specialisation and professionalism were envisioned by Ansari in the 1940s. See Muhammad Yahya, *Uhd Sāz Shakhsiyyat*, 249-51.

the theological institutions (*madāris*). First, his Aligarh years exposed him to the cross-currents of Islamic renewal framed around multidisciplinary knowledge. Furthermore, his postgraduate studies in Islamic theology (*diniyāt*) represented the advanced level of his *Dars i-Nizāmi* background. Second, the cosmopolitan outlook of Mawlana Siddiqui had a significant impact on his formulation of holistic education. His keynote address to the delegates of the Natal Muslim Council (South Africa) in 1952 touched on the nexus between Islamic and secular education. Mawlana Siddiqui clarified this confusion:

> Your religion does not prohibit you from receiving secular education. I say with all the power at my command, that the study of science, philosophy and every branch of education, is open to you and is fully allowed by your religion. You must not differentiate; you must not demarcate between secular and religious and education. You must accept both as being equally necessary.[3]

Without going into the details about the Muslim League and it vision of a separate Muslim homeland, the charismatic leadership of Muhammad Ali Jinnah conceptualised the planning of Muslim education on a national level. It was broad based and aimed at resolving the impasse in the existing system of education among Muslims. The historic appeal by Jinnah elicited well-structured responses from academia. Ansari too, submitted his contributions[4] which outlined the crisis and future planning of Islamic education. Ansari's incisive analysis of the challenges relating to Muslim

---

[3] Cited in Abdul Kader Choughley, *Abdul Aleem Siddiqui and his Mission* (Springs, 2013), 164-5. Cf. Goolam Vahed and Thembisa Waetjen, *Schooling Muslims in Natal. Identity, State and the Orient Islamic Educational Institute* (Pietermaritzburg, 2015), 162-3.

[4] Ansari, *The Present Crisis in Islam and our Future Educational Programme.* Edited by Umair Siddiqui (Karachi, 2017).

Perspectives on the Islamisation of Knowledge

education evolved in his first tabligh travel to Singapore in 1938. `is presentation was firmly grounded in the dynamic formulation of the Islam and knowledge discourse.

The 'throes of a new birth' was a reference to the creation of Pakistan which was in its gestation period. This book was originally an essay written in 1943 and published in 1944, suggesting that Ansari supported the reconfiguration of Islamic education as proposed by Jinnah. He maintained that Muslims needed "to strike the deadliest blows at the defeatist mentality" and extricate themselves from 'intellectual serfdom'.[5] In other words, the inferiority complex had set in so deeply in the mindset of the Muslim intelligentsia that they saw Western education as their only alternative of success. As a result, Islamic education was relegated to the margins and the Muslim community was subsequently deprived of positive idealism.[6] Ansari paints a grim picture of the pervasive influence of Western civilisation in these words:

> The Muslim world is passing through a crisis unprecedented in her history. The crisis has been created by the impact of Western civilisation on the world of Islam. It began when, after enslaving the world politically, the Western imperialist powers planned their subtle strategy of crushing the spirit of cultural self-determination among the Muslims, on the one hand, and of introducing a system of education which aimed at enslaving the Muslim mind, on the other. How hostile and well-designed had been their strategy can be judged even if we consider only the Macaulay Report on educational policy in the British territories, the laws framed by French colonialists for undermining Islam in Africa, and the repressive imperialist policies pursued by Holland in Indonesia.[7]

---

[5] Ibid., 18.
[6] Mohamed, *Islam to the Modern Mind*, 236.
[7] Ansari, *Islam and Western Civilisation*, 3.

In the subcontinent, Lord Macaulay who presided over the education committee set up by the British government was appointed to decide whether education should be imparted to the Indians in their own language or in English. He pleaded for the adoption of the English language in   the following terms: "We must do our best to form a class who may be interpreters between us and the millions whom we are going to govern; a class of persons, Indian in blood and colour, but English in taste, opinions, words and intellect."[8] For Muslims, the strategy was clear: to dislodge the legacy (*turāth*) of the Islamic culture by moulding a class of modernist Muslims to entrench the British educational policy on the Indian soil. In response to the upsurge of the de-Islamising culture, Ansari forcefully supported the Educational Autonomy as it marked a bold reappraisal of the existing Islamic education in the subcontinent.

Muslim intellectual Emancipation and Islamic Reconstruction[9]

Ansari outlines two core issues which have impacted on the Muslim intellectual decline in the twentieth century. First, the enemies of Islam (read as Western civilisation) attributed the inherent flaws in Islam for its intellectual sterility. This contention is baseless as it seeks to dismantle the rich legacy of Islam. Second, the loss of political power had a direct bearing on the Intellectual defeatism in the light of Muslim

---

[8] Adapted from B.D. Basu, *History of Education in India under the Rule of East India Company* (Kolkata, 1930), 87.

[9] The article forms an important chapter of Ansari's *The Present Crisis in Islam*. It is an annotated version which brings into sharp relief the contemporary relevance of issues raised by Ansari in 1943. See Abdul Kader Choughley (ed.), *Moral and Spiritual Transformation in Islam* (Springs, 2019), 190-99.

response to modernism. Amid these political realities, no Muslim countries had contributed "in any appreciable degree to the revival of the Islamic world order."[10] Turkey is an instance in point. After the dissolution of the Ottoman Caliphate in 1923, it embraced Western civilisation in totality. The Kemalist policies were directed at removing any vestige of the Islamic identity which had flourished more than eight hundred years under the Caliphate rule. Likewise, the Muslim world failed to launch a vigorous campaign to restore its former glory. Ansari employed an apt analogy to describe the intellectual fortunes of the Muslim countries: "Our national existence has in consequence come to resemble a tree whose roots have been washed bare by the mighty torrent of Western civilisation. The tree is slowly withering, decaying and collapsing for want of proper nourishment."[11]

In the spirit of objectivity, Ansari brings to the fore the conflicting responses to the incursion of Western civilisation. A growing trend has absorbed shades of grey to highlight the possible compromise between Islamic and Western ideals. In contrast, the general Muslim masses are stuck in a time warp who refuse to acknowledge the dynamic character of Islam. There has been no fundamental mindset shift and this has resulted in the cleavage between Islamic and secular knowledge. In a cynical tone, Ansari deplores the Muslim degeneration in the intellectual domain. It has not produced reformers like Imam Shafi'i, Ghazali and many others. Instead, it has produced charlatans like the blind men of India who went to see an elephant. "The one blind person says that the elephant is like a thick rope, another says it is like a pillar. Are we not doing the same?... The healthy spiritual and intellectual culture does not exist anymore. Neither do the conditions for

---

[10] Ibid., 193

[11] Ibid., 194.

a healthy, moral pattern of life."[12]

According to Ansari, the intellectual renaissance of Islam (*nahdah*) hinges on four fundamental principles:

1. To eliminate all anti-Islamic elements from our intellectual life.
2. To impart to the intellectual aspect of our national existence a true and positive Islamic character by creating a distinct and powerful Islamic thought which may fundamentally cover all branches of knowledge.
3. To ensure and conserve our intellectual self-sufficiency.
4. To bridge up the gulf and resolve the conflict which exists today between theological and 'secular' education as our ancestors did in the heyday of Islamic civilisation. This (approach) will allow Islam the opportunity for its full and rich expression in our intellectual life, which should finally become the bedrock for raising up the mighty edifice of our distinct civilisation.[13]

The guidelines for the Islamic renaissance are expressed in the following words:

The function of this *ummah* will be to unleash all the treasures of knowledge that are buried in the different civilisations of the world: to preserve, to classify and to rectify all the different types of knowledge and advance the cause of knowledge.[14]

---

[12] Mohamed, *Islam to the Modern Mind*, 147.

[13] Ansari, *Moral and Spiritual Transformation in Islam*, 196-7.

[14] Ansari, *Islam to the Modern Mind*, 188.

Islamic Reorientation of Education

It will be worthwhile to examine Ansari's formulation of progressive orthodoxy in the background of the Islamisation of knowledge. He has made reference to a book entitled *The Process of Future Islamic Revolution*[15] which presumably was not published. However, the articles/ chapters generally appear in monographs or are expanded in separate books as is the case with *Islam and Christianity*. Overall, these pieces of writings are comprehensively covered in his major work *The Qur'ānic Foundations*. This term appears to be a self- contradiction on account of the perception associated with orthodoxy or Islamic fundamentalism. In recent decades the myth around 'Islamic formalism' has been debunked by the well-structured studies of Islamic and multidisciplinary knowledge. Ansari may be regarded as among the pioneers who have articulated the Islamisation of knowledge. This is evident from the essay which he contributed to the national education scheme of 1943. More importantly, Ansari gave tangible form to his vision of the Islamisation framework with the establishment of the Aleemiyah Institute of Islamic studies. Essentially, the Institute was not a hybrid model based on a 'patch' work programme but a constructive, well-developed reframing of the *iqrā* paradigm. While Islamic Institutes with impeccable credentials promoted this concept on a global level, Ansari singlehandedly undertook the onerous task within tabligh framework. This, indeed, was his singular achievement.

Ansari critiques Westernised Muslims who influenced by intellectual defeatism are opposed to the idea that Islam is "a discipline, a way of life, a self-contained culture, and a self-sustained civilisation." Because of the complexity of the contemporary Muslim world and the entrenched presence of nationalism following the end of colonial rule, the

---

[15] Ansari, *The Present Crisis in Islam*, 22.

phenomenon of contemporary Islamic thought has been influenced by varied forms of the intellectual trends in South Asia after the Partition of India in 1947. In the case of Indonesia, its intellectual history began after the Independence of the country in 1945.[16] The intellectuals created their own interpretations in which Islam was effectively marginalised. As opposed to the liberal tendencies adopted by Westernised Muslims, Ansari categorically stated that it was only the Islamic teachings which had the 'redeeming powers and infinite possibilities'[17] to lead Muslims to the path of world leadership. Ansari expressed his candour regarding a large segment of Muslims who stiled the creative impulse of the Islamic intellectual spirit and disdained to form contact with modern problems.[18] In response to these bleak situations, he proposed an overhaul of Muslim education in order to initiate the Islamic intellectual renaissance. Ibrahim Abu Rabi` is of the view that the Islamic tradition (*al-turāth al-Islami*) incorporates Islamic resurgence which is interchangeably used for Islamic renaissance. His analysis shares a thematic unity with Ansari's formulation: creating a powerful Islamic thought nurtured in the Islamic ethos and fundamentally covering all branches of knowledge.[19]

It is the process of the Islamisation of knowledge, Ansari maintains, that can successfully achieve the intellectual renaissance project. Two aspects deserve specific mention in this context:

The creation of a Muslim background and Muslim point

---

[16] For a detailed discussion on the Islamic intellectual trends, see Ibrahim Abu-Rabi`, *The Blackwell Companion to Contemporary Islamic Thought* (Oxford, Blackwell Publishing, 2006), 1-20

[17] Kriel, *Islamic Intellectual Revival*, 70.

[18] Ibid.

[19] Ibid., 71-3, Cf. Abu- Rabi, *Intellectual Origins of Islamic Resurgence in the Modern Islamic World* (New York Suny Press, 1996), 55-6.

Perspectives on the Islamisation of Knowledge

of view in subjects taught at Muslim institutions. For example, Philosophy of Religion, Moral Philosophy, Politics, Economics, etc. can be critically studied from the Islamic viewpoint.[20]

The blending of the theological (Islamic) and secular education as the "bedrock for raising up the mighty edifice of our distinct civilisation."[21]

At the heart of the Islamic tradition is the pivotal role of Islamic institutions (*madāris*) as the transmitter of change and continuity within the social and cultural milieu. Over the centuries the madrasah system with its various forms was defined as an institution offering intermediate and advanced instruction in the Islamic tradition. It also provided instruction in secular subjects including astronomy, medicine, philosophy and poetry. Several *madāris* distinguished themselves for training Muslim luminaries including jurists, `ulama, mathematicians and scientists.[22] The Nizamiyah madrasah[23] founded by the Seljuk vizier, Nizam al-Mulk in Baghdad in 1067 represented progressive trends in the Islamic intellectual thought.

In the narrow sense Islamic knowledge was made available to the Muslim society and transmitted to generations by the `ulama. They were transmitters and not priests and "shaped

---

[20] Kriel, *Islamic Intellectual Revival*, 79.

[21] Ibid., 72.

[22] Robert Hefner, *The Culture, Politics and Future of Muslim Education*, in Muhammad Qasim Zaman (eds.) *Schooling Islam* (Princeton, 2007), 5-6. This work is a major contribution to understanding the culture and politics of modern Muslim education in the Muslim world.

[23] The Nizamiyyah madrasah is erroneously assumed to be the first madrasah built in Iraq and Khurasan. There were other *madāris* which existed before its establishment and also received patronage by no less a vizier than Nizam al-Mulk (d. 1092). See Omid Safi, *The Politics of Knowledge in Premodern Islam* (Chapel Hill, 2006), 90-7.

both the outward form and inner nature of Muslim societies."[24] In fact, they were closely associated with *tajdidi* (revivalist) movements[25] and embodied the Qur'ān and sunnah as markers of Islamic authenticity (*turāth*). During the nineteenth century the most active `ulama were those associated with the *tajdidi* tradition of Muslim intellectuals. The widespread efforts to stem the tide of Western civilisation and Muslim conservatism was represented by Syed Jamaluddin Afghani (d.1897).[26] However, during the twentieth century the major Islamic institutions and the `ulama became a deciding conservative force.[27] In South Asia the 'ulama formation was influenced by a colonial past and the emergence of sectarian (*maslak*) divisions.[28]

Ansari's assessment of Islamic institutions is succinctly expressed in his article *Islamic Theological Education*.[29] He regards the `ulama to be the 'heart of the *ummah*'[30] as they are the custodians of the Prophetic knowledge. The ideological community under the leadership of `ulama mirrors progressive intellectual trends and dynamic spiritual values. This nexus has served as a beacon light for the *ummah* over the centuries.[31] Present situations and realities, Ansari contends, have diminished the role of the `ulama as bastions of the Islamic tradition. Consequently, Muslim scholarship proved deficient in fulfilling the needs of the community and

---

[24] Francis Robinson, *Islam, South Asia and the West* (Oxford, 2007), 30.

[25] See Ishtiaq Qureshi, *Ulema in Politics*, 214-39.

[26] Ansari, *Moral and Spiritual Transformation*, 198.

[27] See the writer's analysis on the 'ulama decline with specific reference to South Asia, in Abdul Kader Choughley, *Islamic Resurgence: Sayyid Abul Hasan Ali Nadwi and His Contemporaries* (New Delhi, 2011), 84-96.

[28] Zaman in his magisterial study on the `ulama formation outlines the reasons for the sectarian orientation (*maslak*). See Muhammad Qasim Zaman, *The `Ulama in Contemporary Islam: Custodians of Change.*

[29] Ansari, "Islamic Theological Education: An Urgent Call to the Muslims of the World" in *The Minaret*, 1966, Vol III, No. 6.

[30] Ibid., 2.

[31] Ibid., 5.

this was glaringly evident in the 'two conflicting and mutually hostile systems of thought'[32] that sapped the dynamics of Islamic thought. While acknowledging the contributions of the `ulama, Ansari lamented their failure to recognise the debilitating effects of the separate religious and secular system of education which were in direct contrast to Islam's unitary vision - a fundamental principle of *tawhid*.

In order to remedy the anomalous situation, Ansari proposed the following steps:

The Islamic institutions should adopt a comprehensive course of education incorporating Comparative Religion, and critical study of modern thought. In this way they would be able to establish rationally the truth of the Islamic teachings and their superiority over the teachings of other religions and ideologies.

Spiritual growth and training (*tarbiyat*) should be an integral feature in the curriculum and vigorously pursued in line with the legacy of Muslim luminaries in South Asia and other Muslim countries.

Courses in tabligh should be systematically structured for graduates who wish to devote their energies in this important field.[33]

The concept of *tarbiyat* and *tazkiyah* is a recurrent theme in the writings of Ansari and Mawlana Siddiqui. These terms are value-oriented and provide effective leadership for Muslims to assume their rightful role as *khalifah*. Ansari elucidates:

> The world of Islam will have to revive the pursuit of comprehensive *tazkiyah* in accordance with norms and principles as laid down by the Qur'an and sunnah, in order that the genuine Islamic leadership of the Muhammadan path (*tariqah*) emerges on a high level and in a large

---

[32] Ibid., 4.
[33] Ibid., 6

measure acts fruitfully for the mission of Islam.[34]

All facets of the Holy Prophet's life were fused with spirituality; therefore, it was the inner dimensions that drew man spontaneously and unconditionally to Allah. All actions were directed to earn His pleasure. In this regard Mawlana Siddiqui makes a perceptive comment:

It is the unique and distinguishing feature of the Holy Prophet's character that he was a 'man of the world' and a 'man to Allah' at one at the same time. His devotion to and communion with Allah and the performance of his multifarious duties as the leader of the Faithful, went side by side. He was the human personification of Islam, which combines in its harmonious system the 'religious' as well as the 'secular' aspects of human activity. [It] destroys the very foundation of the popular notion of 'secular things' by supplying a spiritual basis for each and every conceivable aspect of our life.[35]

Islamic Reorientation of Education: An Assessment

A summative assessment of Ansari's envisaged educational reform is given in the light of the historic All India Muslim Educational Conference. Ansari proposed a three-tier system which could remedy the anomaly of Muslim education. The fundamental question raised was the commitment of the different sectors of society to effect meaningful changes. These included the *madāris*, Muslim universities and intellectuals. Of equal importance was the establishment of Muslim schools which could work in tandem to realise the

---

[34] Ansari, *The Qur'ānic Foundations*, vol. 2, 360.

[35] Cited in Choughley, *Abdul Aleem Siddiqui and his Mission*, 199-200.

objectives of the Conference.

Based on the detailed guidelines set out by Ansari, the *madāris* could serve as conduit to implement the ambitious project of Ansari. From the preliminary stages, the merger of Islamic and secular subjects was emphasised. Elementary subjects which were in vogue in the 1940s could be taught alongside Islamic *'ulum*. This was a preparatory phase and could be augmented at both intermediate and advanced levels. Crucial to this proposed change was the guiding spirit of the Qur'ān and sunnah. Most importantly, the structural changes should not compromise the primacy of these key sources of Islam.

According to Ansari, the structured approach for the *madāris* had a transformative ideal: to incorporate Western disciplines framed around the Islamic episteme. In other words, there was to be no grafting of the secular subjects without vetting its contents within the Islamic perspective. Therefore, a monitoring mechanism would ensure its conformity to the Islamic ideals. Ansari conceded that it was a daunting task to overhaul the present madrasah system without incorporating English as a compulsory subject. Additionally, subjects like Economics, Geography, Moral Philosophy, etc. would enhance the *Nizāmi* curriculum.

Ansari also focused on the courses at the universities. For him the transformation project was embedded in higher institutes of learning. Keeping in mind the proposed Islamic state of Pakistan the need for Muslim intellectuals was a priority. Essentially, the courses offered had to exemplify the Islamic ethos. Otherwise, it would produce a defeatist mentality which would be reminiscent of the Muslim modernist worldview, the bane of the Muslim society. On a positive note, Ansari maintained that if Islamic subjects were made compulsory in the academic curriculum then the prospects of nurturing a generation of committed intellectuals working towards the Islamisation project were promising.

The think tank of academic institutions is the research centre. According to Ansari, a well-resourced centre will take the lead in producing a cadre of scholars whose writings will be reflective of the *iqrā* model. The premier universities like AMU and Osmania University had the personnel and resources to conduct research in the new courses like Muslim Philosophy and Islamic history. In fact, the Kemal Yar Jung Committee had passed a resolution for the inclusion of Islamic subjects in Indian universities and the establishment of a central research organisation under the auspices of the Committee. Ansari was familiar with the intellectual trends in the country and strongly advocated the restructuring of Islamic courses. For example, he made an impassioned appeal for the production of textbooks that were aligned to the Islamic ideals. Likewise, he lamented the lacuna of scholarly works in these fields which could replace the Orientalist works. Their bias and 'unscientific malevolence' was ingrained in their writings with the result that they moulded a generation of Muslim scholars to promote their deviant interpretation of Islamic history. Muslim indifference to the political history of Islam covering the early Caliphate, Abbasid dynasty, Ottoman caliphate, etc. was a contributing factor to the misrepresentation by these Orientalists of Islam's rich legacy. More disturbing was the lack of knowledge regarding Muslim nations in China, Russia, East Indies and Africa. This lamentable situation could be addressed by accredited Muslim research academies. In sum, standards of excellence in the Islamic and secular domains were pre-requisites for the genuine transformation of Muslim education.[36]

In his perceptive article, *The Problem of Islamic Research*[37] Ansari develops his arguments regarding the sinister designs

---

[36] See Ansari, *The Present Crisis in Islam*, 70-91. The important aspects have been gleaned from the book.

[37] The article was published in *The Voice of Islam*. Vol. 3: 12, September 1955.

of the Orientalist writings which have percolated courses offered in the different universities of India and Pakistan since 1928. In contrast, there have been no substantive intellectual contributions, particularly in the case of the 'History of Muslim Philosophy'. No Muslim institution or philanthropist has sponsored a feasible project to the promotion of an instructive course like Muslim philosophy. Ansari's analysis of the Orientalist project is illustrative:

> Western scholarship on Islam, as manifested in the writings of the Orientalists, has pursued its own pre-planned course from the very beginning. Islamic research was instituted in Western countries not to arrive at truth on the basis of intellectual honesty but to serve ulterior ends. Consequently, the work of the Orientalists has been marred throughout with an unscientific malevolence and an intellectual dishonesty which has known no bounds. Of course, there have been certain honourable exceptions too. But they have been so few as to be incapable of changing the course of Orientalist scholarship.[38]

Pioneers of Islamisation of Contemporary Knowledge

There have been several influential Muslim figures who have made noteworthy contributions to the Islamisation of knowledge project. Ismail Raji Faruqi (d. 1986) established the International Institute of Islamic Thought (IIIT) in 1981. His famous monograph entitled *The Islamisation of Knowledge* was the starting point of developing a well-formulated interpretation of the multidisciplines through the prism of *tawhid*. In Malaysia, it is Syed Naquib Al-Attas (b. 1931) who considers the Qur'an and Nature as open Books, except that the former is

---

[38] Ansari, *The Beacon Light*, 351.

uncreated. In this perspective, he strongly maintains that the traditional methods of understanding the Qur'an through *tafsir* and *ta'wil* without succumbing to apologetics are the benchmark of giving contemporary knowledge a distinctly Islamic character. In this regard Wan Daud states that "the solutions that Al-Attas have been consistently proposing are neither merely to devise ways and means to accommodate modern Western scientific spirit through a reinterpretation of Islam..."[39] In other words, it would be naïve to import Western technological skills and products to support Qur'anic truths. On the contrary, Islam possesses within itself the source of its claim to truth, and does not need scientific theories to justify such a claim.

Ansari's formulation of the Islamisation project has not received critical examination for several reasons. First, there was a time gap of almost twenty years (1944-64) before he could implement his educational reform. Second, it was an individual effort to undertake such a daunting task. Third, his vision was framed around the tabligh discourse. Notwithstanding the limitations of his reform plans, he succeeded in establishing the Aleemiyah Institute for this purpose.

The 'pursuit of excellence' is a recurrent theme in the Islamic knowledge discourse. According to Ansari, the Holy Prophet (SAW) emphasised the fact that the pursuit of knowledge should be anchored on observation and acceptable scientific methodology. Therefore, the mission of the Muslim community is three-fold: conquest of the self, social environment and nature. In this respect, the spirit of Islam invites man to develop the realisation of God (*ma'rifah*) through the pursuit of knowledge. In this perspective, the study of the phenomena of nature is encapsulated in the following verse:

---

[39] Wan Mohd Nor Wan Daud, *The Educational Philosophy and Practice of Syed Muhammad Naquib Al-Attas* (Kuala Lumpur, 1998), 376.

Those who truly fear Allah are among His servants who have knowledge. For Allah is exalted in Might, Oft-Forgiving. (35: 28)

Thus, the Holy Prophet (SAW) not only stated that it was act of *'ibādah* for his fellowmen but he also charted the course of science. If you read the works on the history of science which are largely written by non-Muslim scholars you will note their pertinent remarks that physical science before the advent of the Holy Prophet (SAW) was pre-scientific. The deductive method was already known to the Greeks who organised, systematised and channelised knowledge. In contrast to this form of knowledge, the inductive method was unknown to the Indian, Greek and Chinese civilisations. In fact, the history of science acknowledges the contributions of the Holy Prophet (SAW) and his fellowmen for promoting the inductive method of enquiry.[40]

Iqbal and Ansari: Shared Vision

Ansari held Iqbal in great esteem and was deeply impressed by his vision of Islamic renewal. In the domain of intellectual legacy, he supported Iqbal's articulation of fusing knowledge within this framework. A closer reading of *The Reconstruction of Religious Though*[41] reveals the underpinnings of Iqbal's reformist thought. In fact, Ansari has cited a lengthy passage from this work in his *The Qur'ānic Foundations* to describe the predicament of modern man who "overshadowed by his intellectual activity

---

[40] Ansari, *Moral and Spiritual Transformation in Islam*, 170.

[41] Muhammad Iqbal, *The Reconstruction of Religious Thought in Islam* (Lahore, 1971). It is a compilation of six lectures which were delivered in Madras (Chennai), Hyderabad and Aligarh. The book was brought out in 1930. Iqbal's philosophical background is visible in these lectures which have a reformist thrust.

has ceased to live soulfully i.e. from within."[42] As a result, the moral and spiritual turmoil has deprived him of leading a meaningful life. Iqbal's critique of modern philosophy is endorsed by Ansari's well-developed arguments about the cleavage caused by these theories that militate against Islam's universal teachings. Against the doom and gloom syndrome, Iqbal's soul-stirring message of faith rings across the world of Islam:

- Faith consists in forsaking one's ego and living in the ecstasy of Divine presence
- Faith consists in accepting the ordeal of fire like Ibrahim
- Listen! O you who have been enthralled by modern civilization
- The lack of faith is worse than political slavery.[43]

According to Ansari, the pursuit of knowledge has divine sanction. It dispels the layers of ignorance and superstition cast in the mould of the *Jahiliyyah* age. With the advent of Islam, the world was the beneficiary of enlightenment and scientific enquiry. While other faiths like Christianity wallowed in medieval darkness, it was Islam that ushered in a new world order. When Muslims lost their prestige and civilisational role, the European renaissance took a lead in influencing the realms of science and technology. However, it was devoid of religious consciousness. Again, Ansari reiterates the dynamism of the *iqrā* model to extricate mankind from the scourge of materialism. Muslims are reminded of their unconditional commitment to the following declaration:

Back to Allah, the Author of our existence, the Author of

---

[42] Ibid., 187-8.
[43] Ansari, *The Present Crisis in Islam*, 96.

Islam, the Author of the Universe/Back to the Qur'anic stream of perennial life and light/Back to the world-leader Muhammad (SAW).[44]

---

44 Ibid., 97.

CHAPTER 6

Science and Religion Discourse:
Ansari's Assessment

After Ansari graduated with an MA in philosophy at AMU in 1942, his writings in this field grew in stature and importance. Interestingly, the depth and maturity of his philosophical works are succinctly expressed in a number of articles and essays as well as monographs.

In this chapter the formulation of moral philosophy as a subset of Islamic philosophy is examined. Under the rubric of the science and religion discourse, Ansari's contributions are compared with his two illustrious mentors, Mawlana Siddiqui and Syed Zafarul Islam, both of whom are discussed in Chapter 1. The commonality of Ansari and Mawlana Siddiqui's exposition in this field is indeed remarkable. Both were distinguished ʿulama who sought to recast Islamic thought in modern idiom. Their respective Islamic worldview was framed around the emerging trends of modern science, philosophy and theory of religion. In the chapter, *Religion, science and development* Alladin has given an overview of Mawlana Siddiqui's lecture which was delivered at the M. K. Gandhi Hall (Durban, South Africa) in 1936. The topic was on "The Religious and Scientific progress of the World." The academic community was held spellbound by his profound views and exposition.

According to Mawlana Siddiqui, the myths built around science and religion as two mutually exclusive entities were largely caused by scientists who rejected the notion of the religious element in their scientific world. Conversely, the religious sector had no reason to be averse to natural science for elucidating the problems of theology. Rather, a reciprocal relationship should be struck up to expand the horizon of the scientific spirit harnessed in a religious environment. This nurturing process would alleviate the plight of humanity and give a sense of purpose in all spheres of life. A fundamental question that has preoccupied philosophers is the existence of a Creator of the universe. For Mawlana Siddiqui, it is a universal belief that defies the logic of philosophers or rationalists whose conclusions on the nature of creation are tendentious, to say the least. Mawlana Siddiqui draws upon the sources of the existing researches to counter the arguments of these dubious claims. Likewise, he is able to demonstrate the incongruity of these findings by referring to eminent scientists and philosophers whose belief in the Supreme Power has provided a deep sense of communion beyond the ken of reason. In fact, the language of the sacred assumes greater significance in the lives of a believer who is unencumbered by the philosophy overload. In his view "the function of religion is to direct the cultivation of love for the Creator, and thereby bring such moral elevation that one may become a veritable personification of sublime morals." It is Islam that promotes equilibrium (*i'tidal*) in societal life through its universal teachings.[1]

In his incisive exposition of the philosophical underpinnings of creation, Ansari adduces scientific proof to counter the theories which in his view are untenable. In his discussion about the grades of creation, Ansari ably demonstrates the Islamic concept of the universe and the purpose of life. These are not arbitrary play of forces or random acts of creation but built around a divine scheme that is perfect and suited to human conditions. Accordingly, man's position in the universe is derived from the Islamic view of life. There exists no contradiction between material and spiritual dimensions of life; therefore, the realisation of Divine pleasure is accorded

---

[1] Alladin, *Maulana Abdul Aleem Siddiqui*, 183-207 (Adapted).

Science and Religion Discourse:
Ansari's Assessment

the status of worship (*'ibādah*).[2]

Transcendental issues are deftly woven into a rational interpretation of Islamic doctrines by Ansari. For example, death is referred to as *intiqāl* or transfer from one state of existence to another. Hence the Islamic doctrines concerning the nature of death, continuity of life, resurrection and the Afterlife have full support in human experience. According to Ansari, the Qur'an has declared the forms of life the soul has experienced before creation. In other words, there is an inseparable link in man's life beyond death. The phenomenon of human growth resembles the evolution of man's transfer from one form to another form, which negates the theory of annihilation advanced by skeptics. Their mindset is no different from the disbelievers who rejected resurrection as clearly stated in the Qur'ān. In this case, the materialistic-leaning disbelievers are offered rational explanation concerning the Islamic viewpoint of eschatology. Ansari reaffirms the true contents of faith without deviating from the mainstream interpretation of Islamic doctrines. His thorough grounding in philosophy and other related disciplines placed him in a unique position to unravel the rationale of Islamic teachings.[3]

In Ansari's perspective, philosophical and scientific discussions have no merit if these are not guided by religious guidance.

He explains: Divine guidance, according to Islam has been universal. Adam was the first man and also the first Prophet of God. After him guidance continued to come from God to all the communities and countries of the world. The Holy Qur'an says: *Every people had a guide.* (13: 7)

---

[2] Ansari, "Grades in Creation" in *The Muslim Digest*, June 1969, 5-9.
[3] Ansari, "Foundations of Faith" in *The Beacon Light*, 42-75. Cf. Ansari, "What is the Real Heaven?" in *The Muslim Digest* (1945), 57-65.

This guidance was fundamentally the same because it came from one God and it came to the whole humanity. Though the same in its fundamentals, it was at that time evolutionary, expanding and developing in scope as the vast human communities progressed from a lower stage of culture and civilisation to a higher one, until when humanity was finalised, matured and perfected in the Divine guidance in the form of the Holy Qur'an to the Holy Prophet Muhammad (SAW). He is the last and greatest Messenger of God. As regards the Holy Qur'an, it is not only the last Book but also the only one which exists without any interpolation or change up to this day.[4]

Syed Zafarul Hasan was a remarkable academic on two counts. First, he was among the pioneers who developed a distinct school of philosophy possessing unmissable traits of the Islamic tradition. Second, he influenced a generation of Muslim scholars who immensely enriched the multidisciplinary facets of philosophy. In more ways than one, Ansari was ranked among his outstanding students who produced cutting-edge scholarship to his research project. For almost four years he worked on his dissertation under Syed Zafarul's supervision to develop new perspectives on the theory of Moral Philosophy. The circumstances of his 'labour of love' are briefly recounted in Chapter 1.

In his address to students of philosophy organised by the Philosophical Society of AMU (Ansari also served as its President) in 1931, Syed Zafarul Hasan provided the Islamic perspective on the nature, scope and function of this important discipline. He maintained that philosophy covered the intellectual domain and was interlinked with the Qur'anic concept of *hikmah* (wisdom). Two strands of philosophy,

---

[4] Ibid., 57-8.

Science and Religion Discourse:
Ansari's Assessment

theoretical and practical, were woven around the overarching vision of Moral Philosophy. It was an intensive study undertaken by Ansari for his doctoral dissertation. According to Syed Zafarul Hasan, Islam infused new life into philosophy by articulating the centrality of ethics (*akhlāq*) and other disciplines within the Qur'anic purview. In other words, the Islamic philosophical content permeated a diverse range of subjects which was influenced by the broad definition of *hikmah*. For example, philosophers like Ghazali and poets like Rumi contributed immensely to the Islamic tradition of philosophy through their celebrated writings. In a similar vein, many Muslim poets couched their creative genius through the language of philosophy, which was anchored on the Islamic ideals.[5]

We now focus on Syed Zafarul Hasan's explanation of revelation (*wahy*) within a philosophical framework. The choice of language is persuasive, lucidly expressed and boldly stated.

Then look at the Message which the Prophets brought for man - a reply to that great question which was making his soul restless and which reason had failed to solve. An answer so clear, so distinct, so satisfying - did it come from anywhere else than the great Beyond? It was revelation from which the world learnt what I am and from where I come and where to I am going; and, consequently, what I ought to do and what I ought to become. In other words, it was revelation which told man that there is a Being full of perfection, and that He has brought man and the Universe into being from nothing. It is His will that I should attain perfection. I ought to act according to His

---

[5] Syed Zafarul Hasan, "Philosophy and the Advantages of Studying it" *in Iqbal Review*. April, 2006: 30-45 (Adapted).

will. I ought to become what He requires me to become. I shall have to go in His Presence and I shall have to account for my deeds. On that day if He looks at me with approval, what an attainment! Otherwise, it would be the most patent failure.[6]

Ansari makes a perceptive comment on the status of *wahy* as a source of guidance:

Islam emphasises this all-important fact of revelation. It affirms the existence of God and says that He is the Creator and Cherisher of the Universe. Also, that He is All-Powerful, All- Knowing and Omnipresent. He possesses perfect knowledge of the origin, the constitution and the function of everything, and His knowledge comprehends the past, the present and the future. And He not only possesses that knowledge but He also revealed to humanity the correct guidance on the ultimate and intricate problems which defy correct and sure solution by means and senses of reason. His Revelation came, much like the distant planets mentioned in the foregoing scientific argument, through spiritual luminaries who appeared on the horizon of humanity from time to time. Those spiritual luminaries included men like Adam, Abraham, Moses, Jesus, the last among them being Muhammad (Divine Peace and Blessings be with him and all other Messengers of God); and the last revealed book is the Holy Qur'ān.[7]

The above extracts are representative of their deep reflections on the varied aspects of the sacred text. Without venturing into the domain of philosophical concepts, Syed Zafarul Hasan and Ansari have explored the phenomenon of

---

[6] Syed Zafarul Hasan, *Why Religion* (Karachi, 1976), 5-6.
[7] Ansari, *Through Science and Philosophy to Religion* (Karachi, 1976), 16.

wahy as irrefutable proof of the Qur'an's divine origin. Likewise, several Qur'anic themes are developed around the nature, scope and function of philosophy. What emerges from their respective elucidation of religion are the Qur'anic doctrines of universal divine guidance and unity of religious truth. According to Ansari, the structure of religious creed has an ethical and religious perspective. For example, belief in all the Prophets " is related to the Qur'anic teaching that God being one, and mankind being one, the Guidance of God has come to all the human communities since the time of Adam (peace be upon him) through the Prophets of God. and it has not been confined to any people (because) the Philosophy and the way of submission to God is the same... and where there are resemblances in the teachings of the different religions, they are the remnants of the original Truth revealed by God."[8]

In sum, Ansari draws upon his extensive study of philosophy to press home an important point: Islam provides the universal guidance for mankind. It must be borne in mind that only a brief comment on Ansari's philosophical contribution has been covered. Otherwise, it requires specialised knowledge to document the depth of his knowledge on this discipline. A cursory view of his exposition of the pillars of Islam takes into account the different levels of consciousness which are linked with moral development.[9] Thus the philosophical concepts are simplified and integrated into the cosmos of *'ibādah* - a thoughtful presentation which marks out Ansari as an outstanding Muslim philosopher of the twentieth century. To date, there has been no systematic study of his merit- worthy

---

[8] Ansari, *The Qur'anic Foundations*, vol. 1, 140.
[9] Ansari, *Islam: An Introduction* (Springs, 2019), 59-63.

contributions to the Islamic philosophy tradition.

CHAPTER 7

Facets of Islamic Civilisation

The following articles were published in the *Fifth Pillar*, a quarterly magazine published by Mohammad Makki, editor of *Ramadan Annual* (South Africa). These pieces of writing were written in 1945 after Ansari had completed his MA in Philosophy. To date, these articles have not appeared in any of Ansari's works.

Islamic Beliefs, Practices and Morals

Our Muslim brethren must realise that it is nothing short of heresy not to make the cardinal beliefs in Islam - belief in the one Almighty God with unique attributes, the existence of angels, the Prophets, the Day of Judgement and the divine source of all powers of action – permeate the very bone and marrow of their being and become their virtual principles at all times. A true Muslim must feel   that his thoughts, words and deeds, overt or covert, are witnessed by God, preserved by His mysterious powers and are to be accounted for on the Day of Judgement. These burning religious sentiments begin to be responsible for the maintenance of perfect law and order in Muslim society without the necessity of any police, some thirteen hundred years ago. Every true Muslim should have, and has, the same feelings. But the hypocrite, who under the cloak of 'Muslim', is in reality anything but Muslim. He does not, of course, care for such Islamic principles, and brings, through his un-Islamic ways, disgrace to the unsullied Muslim community to which he professedly belongs. Alas, how long the Muslim community has to tolerate such wolves in sheep's clothing, we cannot say. We pray that such people would realise this grave situation and improve themselves. So much for the beliefs, just now.

Now for the actions: no Muslim should be ignorant of the great philosophical significance of the Islamic fundamental practices and the wonderful benefits accruing from their observance. Muslims, of course, know the five pillars of Islam. Yet there are Muslims who neglect to carry out these very fundamental actions faithfully and they cherish the notion that they too are good Muslims. Read the Qur'ān and note the number of repetitions peremptorily commanding the regular observance of these. Read the hadith and shudder at the harsh tones at those who breach these observances (pillars of Islam) are condemned as outside the pale of Islam – and then judge whether you can be successful spiritually, if you don't translate these commandments conscientiously into practice. Can anyone who is too slothful, too undisciplined and too unmannered to observe these emphatically commanded fundamental practices of Islam hope to be reverent or to be a faithful follower of Islam and the Prophet? Materialism and Western civilisation are blinding the eyes of some Muslims too much to observe the beauty of these practices. Let the so- called 'educated' Muslims realise that the file pillars of Islam are the irreducible minimum that Islam demands of every one of its followers.

It is the duty of every Muslim to study the Islamic injunctions clearly given in respect of moral qualities. Piety, cleanliness, charity, brotherly affection, love, truthfulness, chastity, honesty, humility, patience, perseverance, punctuality, etc. are inculcated in the most emphatic and convincing manner by Islam and every Muslim should be an embodiment of all these qualities and make all his thoughts, words and deeds conform to these. Only those who do so can claim to be really good Muslims; others are hypocrites and are chaff deserving to be cast away from the Islamic society.

Conversely, those who drink or use any toxicant in any form, those who commit adultery and commit breach of trust or cheat in any way, those who slander, those who hoard wealth without putting it in any beneficial use, those who create division among their own brotherhood or the general public, etc. – these are the people who openly revolt against the teachings of Islam are its enemies. To be a good Muslim one should persevere and persevere, shun all that is evil and develop all good qualities. Light-headed and light- hearted people, calling themselves Muslims, think, speak and act as they please without caring whether they are in accord with the teachings of Islam or not are the worst hypocrites. Will they stop and think awhile, if they wish to remain the followers of Islam and want salvation?[1]

Muslim Societies: Whither Civilisation Leads Today?

From the self-centred and segregated family life of primitive man, man's mode of living has gradually developed, each successive stage of civilisation showing that he ought more and more to become less selfish in his outlook on life and train himself for a family, communal, racial, national and international viewpoint in his dealing with others. From his isolated family life, he thus emerged into family life; and then to urban life. In the course of time he trained himself to live a nationally corporate life. Twentieth century civilisation culminated in international co-operation and solidarity. Internationalism is certainly the most praiseworthy ideal of civilised life. To recede from such civilised outlook cannot but push us back to more primitive types of society. The intelligent man is convinced today that internationalism is therefore higher and more beneficial to humanity than narrow-minded and trouble- brewing nationalism. Should all people generally realise this, the world would soon near the millennium, making it a happier and secure place for all men

---

[1] Ansari, "Islamic Beliefs, Practices and Morals", *Fifth Pillar* (1945), 71-5.

to live in. The recent war (World War II) and the resultant dismal cloud that overhangs the world bears eloquent testimony to the supreme necessity of men becoming more tolerant towards their fellow men and upholding an international outlook on all their dealings.

While political gamblers might revert from one phase to another, the general public is firm in clinging fast to the spirit of unity. All over the world we find societies of all classes, from the manual labourers to the highest intellectuals going heart and soul for international unions, federations and societies. They have been convinced of the superior merits and the invaluable benefits accruing from united efforts. Whoever hears of international labour unions advocating reversion to isolated groups? How much more should we expect the intellectual classes to fight tooth and nail for unity in these days?

What the twentieth century attempted in the League of Nations, Islam had accomplished in the obligatory gathering of all nations of the earth at Makkah, thirteen hundred years ago. This League of Nations spirit is based on the Islamic concept of the universal brotherhood. All men are the sons of Adam and all Muslims brothers to one another. Its civilising teaching meant that the Muslims have to cast away the notions of *Jāhiliyyah* and foster the culture of brotherhood in spirit and in practice. All the Islamic institutions and offices were based on merit and goodness. If a Muslim, no matter what his race was, be he a Quraish or an Abyssinian, was better and more deserving of anything, he was to be given preference over anyone else of whatever nationality. Islam knows no narrow- minded nationalism. Islam came to weld different races into one international whole.

The Holy Prophet (SAW) himself put this tenet of Islam into rigid practice. He made an emancipated slave, the leader of a Muslim army consisting of proud and able Quraish leaders. The traditional Quraish pride was wounded too deeply to submit to this "injustice" even at the hands of the Prophet (SAW). A severe reprimand from the Prophet at once made Muslims set aside all distinctions of colour. Again, the Prophet (SAW) gave his own cousin, a high-born Quraish lady in marriage to the emancipated slave. Was any other action more capable of driving home to the Muslims the complete denial of Islam of colour distinctions to any of its followers? Bilal the revered *mu'addhin* of Islam, was but a slave. Who was Salman Fārsi? Later Islamic history, too, abounds in actual instances of the low born becoming rulers, generals, professors, muftis and holders of other high offices. From the very inception of the Islamic society, Islam has known no distinction of nationality or race among its followers. Go to any mosque or any religious gathering, go to any social gathering, to any Islamic institution and examine the records of any such thing of any generation of Muslims and see if ever Islam has shown any discriminating policy. Examine the verses of the Holy Qur'an, scrutinise the sayings of the Prophet (SAW), study the preaching of any Muslim Imam, philosopher, professor, leader or patriot and you will be satisfied that what they all preached was internationalism and Islamism and not nationalism. It means serving towards the selfish advancement, independence, segregation, pride and expansion of one's own geographically-defined nationality and not towards the benefit of all Muslims forming the Islamic brotherhood and race and ignoring their welfare and their share in our prosperity. Even to a man of the meanest intelligence, it will be clear, then, that the noble ideal of Islam was one of a higher, a more humanising and a grander civilisation than the mean conception of a lowly nationalism.

As I have stated above, the saner and the more enlightened of the people of the world are working for international federations, unions, leagues and clubs. The Rotary International is growing in strength day by day. Truly such movements should by their very nature have been championed by Muslims. Each backward Muslim nation should redouble its efforts to come up and surpass others of their brethren in every field of activity. Islam thus encourages healthy rivalry and progress. But what do we find today among certain Muslims, nay, many Muslims of today? Islam has its own civilisation which can hold proudly its own against any other in the world. And yet, as a result of the irony of fate, many have not understood the noble place of Islamic culture and civilisation in the history of the world. Receiving no Islamic education, the resplendent glory of Islam is a closed door to these miserably purblind souls. Alas! Instead of seeking the remedy in the right direction and striving to get light, they begin to advocate alien thoughts and cults, which, as I have exposed above, fall far short of their own Islamic ideals. Instead of giving them peace, happiness and progress as the Islamic ideal proffers, only misconceptions of things lie in the higher Islamic education, the kind to be had at the Al-Azhar of Cairo, the Osmania University of Hyderabad, the Aligarh Muslim University of Aligarh, India, etc.

Muslim clubs, societies, associations, leagues and what not – are legion in every district. Often several such clubs and associations have the same objects and aims and each is run absolutely independently of any other. A great deal of money and energy of Muslims are unnecessarily wasted in such duplicating activities. Where rent and staff expenses for one organisation should be sufficient half-a- dozen societies exist. Amalgamation of such societies with various sub-committees each with its own secretaries with powers to manage their own sections, independent of other sub-committees would go a long way to cement Muslim unity. I appeal to the Muslims of all countries, seriously and in true Islamic spirit, to serve the cause of unity among Muslims by amalgamating societies having identical objects and aims, situated in different towns of one country under the jurisdiction of a central society in the capital town of the whole country.[2]

Prophet Muhammad as the Inaugurator of the Science of Sociology

It is a common assertion that Comte was the first thinker who founded the science of sociology. But this point of view is not corroborated by the facts of the history of social thought. The European historians now openly admit their inferential mistake. Toynbee and Sorokin, the most modern authorities in historicism and social philosophy, on the one hand, and the Orientalists with Ibn Khaldun (d.1406) as their field of enquiry, on the other, admit that about more than six hundred years before Comte, it was Ibn Khaldun who discovered some of the laws, principles and procedures of modern sociology. He propounded some of the theories which stand valid even today: for instance, the theories of space-time causality and micro - and macro-sociological approaches. Among these disciplines the sociology of knowledge, religion and education are notable. The one discovered by Ibn Khaldun, the sociology of metaphysics, is still unknown to the modern sociologists.

Social thoughts are the common legacy of mankind. Their history is traceable since 400 B.C. But these thoughts were never systematised in terms of the knowledge-system. The first comprehensive scientific approach to the science of sociology was presented in the Qur'ān which the Holy Prophet (SAW) delivered to humanity. Under the divine revelation (*wahy*), and inspired by the sociological thought patterns of the Qur'an, the Muslim thinkers took the initiative to formulate them into a definitive system of knowledge supported by other systems of knowledge like humanities, physical sciences

---

[2] "Muslim Societies: Whither Civilisation Leads Today?" in *Fifth Pillar* (1945). Page 45-8.

and sciences called by German thinkers as Geistes Wissenschaften or spiritual sciences. Under these circumstances, it was not possible to isolate sociology from philosophy or theology. Kindi, Farabi, Ibn Miskawayh and a host of others are the predecessors of Ibn Khaldun. He was, however, the person who systematised and synthesised this useful science, giving it the shape of a system of knowledge.

The process of systematisation involves four things:

- Depth and level approach.
- Social determination of thought.
- Scientific procedure i.e. empirical study, critical vision and thought.
- Unitary concept of life.

In the first category the Qur'anic terms like *tafakkur* (contemplation) and *tanzur* (perception) lead us to where the constant reference of each thing created, seen or unseen, is full of meanings. The object of man's superiority over all created things is determined by an axiom that he was created to worship God. One of the sources of realisation to this end is the constant struggle to control nature in the pursuit of knowledge. These form the basis of society and culture. Likewise, words like *sam'a* (hearing) and *basar* (hearing) lead us to infer that these are embedded in empirical scientific methodology covering areas of deduction, induction, experiment, etc. In the all-embracing term of *tawhid* the very idea of the totality and unity of life is covered. It is the basis, or more accurately, the source of all value systems. It is meaningfully related to the Attributes of God, which are ninety-nine in number. These attributes are to be designed as different types of values or amalgamated into one composite whole. Thus, it is the principle of *tawhid* which forms the major premise of the Islamic culture and social order. Within the framework of these attributes, it is possible to determine human typology. Therefore, these attributes like `aleem (knowing) and *habeeb* (loving) are essentially derived from knowledge and experience. Any deviancy has been condemned in terms of sealing of the mind, hearing and seeing- in short, the definitive form of the decay of the person.

In the modern age, it is said that culture is the result of the meaningful orientation and combination of the systems of religion and truth, knowledge and philosophy. The Qur'ān believes in the system of knowledge in its philosophical and simple framework of reference. Thus, the Qur'anic theory of knowledge as analysed in the story of Adam is the story of the sociology of knowledge. Adam was born in a social atmosphere and hence the endowed knowledge (*asmr'*) develops in its right socio-cultural surroundings. Knowledge thus developed, fruitfully acts and reacts on society and gives momentum to culture in the right direction. As a corollary, knowledge dislocated from its central message is no knowledge at all. In this perspective, religion according to the Qur'ān reflects the totality of life: a blending of harmony and solidarity.

Culture has four constituents which are in conformity with the Qur'anic principles of sociology. Any imbalance leads to the dislocation of the system as is evident in the inherent cultural mentality of the West. In contrast, the Qur'anic sociology developed as an interdependent science of different fields of scholarship by different Muslim thinkers and given an exclusive shape by Ibn Khaldun. However, it did not make progress until it was revived by Shah Waliyullah of Delhi. He added new disciplines to it. His *Hujjat Allah al-Bāligha* is his significant contribution to this discipline.

This cursory account of the Qur'anic sociology is simply meant to invite the best inquisitive minds both in the East and the West to pay their due attention to a field which has been neglected and to acknowledge the truth that it was no other than the Holy Prophet (SAW) who inaugurated the first comprehensive scientific approach to the problems of sociology.[3]

---

[3] Reproduced from *The Muslim Digest*, July 1963, 2-6 (Adapted).

Conclusion

A work of this scope has not been an easy task in view of the paucity of material and the timeline of Ansari's academic pursuit in Aligarh Muslim University. It was a formative period of the nascent university seeking to establish its prestige in the subcontinent. The significant strides made in humanities and Islamic studies are illustrative of the trajectory of academic excellence that was built on visionary leadership, Muslim identity and national pride.

Broadly speaking, the writings of Ansari deal with the multiple issues and challenges Muslims were faced with in their quest for Islamic authenticity. AMU provided Ansari the platform to articulate his brilliant exposition of Islam as a complete way of life (*din*). His writings mirrored his multidimensional character: research scholar and *muballigh*. Interestingly, Ansari was able to write on several topics which were wide and varied. It appears that several books belonging to different disciplines were brought out in the same year. His *A New Muslim World in the Making* and *Muhammad The Glory of the Ages* are representative of this time frame. However, these works were published at a later date by organisations which were associated with Mawlana Siddiqui in Kenya and Singapore. In a similar vein, Ansari's articles were brought out by Islamic magazines. In the case of *Genuine Islam* he served as its editor. This partly explains why a few of his monographs were not available in the subcontinent.

Ansari was placed in a unique situation to frame his extensive studies from the lens of tabligh. His 'missionary' travels as was glibly described in the Western media wielded considerable influence concerning Islam's universal role. At the heart of Ansari's vision of tabligh was the synergy of knowledge and spirituality. The moral decline that had eroded religious consciousness could be attributed to the pervasive influence of materialism. Marxism, Communism and Capitalism were offshoots of the materialistic worldview that relegated the universal values of Islam to the margins. Shorn of apologia and polemics, Ansari presented a cogent critique on these ideological systems. In more than one way, they were deemed as existential threats for mankind. Likewise, his deep reflections on the flawed interpretations of religion in the main by philosophers and scientists spurred him to offer a rational interpretation of Islamic culture and civilisation. According to Ansari, revealed religion like Islam offered a shari`ah that was not time and culture specific. Rather, the mainstay of mankind's happiness lay in following the divine prescriptions as outlined by the Holy Prophet (SAW). The imprints of Syed Zafarul Hasan's erudition were visible in Ansari's cosmopolitan outlook on philosophical matters.

Two attributes set Ansari apart from his peers: research and reverence. His research output was remarkable as can be gleaned from his *Communist Challenge to Islam.* The references are extensive and are reflective of Ansari's historical acumen. Likewise, his monograph *Foundations of Faith* brings in different dimensions of philosophical thought. These works are well-structured and bear the hallmarks of enviable scholarship. Apart from his spiritual affiliation with Mawlana Siddiqui, Ansari held in high esteem scholars like Sayyid Sulayman Nadwi and Mawlana Abdul Majid Daryabadi. His correspondence with and reliance on their scholarly contributions mark his sense of reverence. Unassuming in his ways and dyed in the Islamic tradition of *adab* (decorum), Ansari embodied the ideals of the *iqrā* model. In a particular sense, AMU created the academic ambience for brilliant scholars like Ansari to grow and nurture their potentials in the cause of Islam.

Appendix
Appendix 1: Literary Contributions

Mohammed an Ideal Reformer
By Hafiz Mohammed Fazlur Rehman Ansari B.A. (Alig.)
II

(2) The erroneous conception of human dignity: slavery—Muhammad's reforms:—

No social, moral, intellectual and even spiritual evolution is possible in a community which does not possess a true estimate of human dignity, and this was the state of affairs when Muhammad appeared. The dignity and powers of man had been greatly underestimated and undermined by the great religions and cultures of the world. Human dignity had been assailed by various religions and cultural institutions like caste system, serfdom and slavery. It was believed that men and women, those noblest creatures of God, were incapable of leading upright lives in the midst of society, and should therefore become hermits, monks and nuns and lead a life of celibacy and detachment from the world. Buddhism, Hinduism, Zoroastrianism, Confucianism, Jainism, Judaism and Christianity, all believed in this theory. Christianity preached the Sin-innate theory—that corollary of the theory of atonement—, and insisted that man was incapable of observing the law.

When Muhammad appeared to reform the world, he exposed the baselessness of such notions. He declared that human species was the noblest creation of God, and that all things of the universe were created for its use. He asserted that sin is anacquisition and not a heritage (Koran XXX:30) and that man has been endowed with the highest capabilities (Ibid XCV) of achieving unlimited progress if he follows the right path failing which he can also sink to the "lowest of the low (Ibid XCV). He called man by the honourable title of the vicegerent of God on earth (Ibid 11:30)

He preached the unity and equality of mankind and broke the fetters of slavery and caste.

It is trite objection of the opponents of Islam that Muhammad permitted and established the institution of slavery. Nothing more mischievous than this can be conceived.

The institution had been existing since times immemorial. Religion after religion rose but none of them tried to abolish this cruel practice. For the sake of example we may take the case of Christianity, which is one of the great religions of the world and whose missioraries and ministers are highly fond of attacking Islam in season and out of season.

Christianity flourished in the Roman Empire where, though slavery had been a recognised institution for centuries, men like Dis Chrysostom, Diocletian and Scenca had begun to protest against the cruel practice. But the work of reform was checked at its very outset by Christianity. This fact might surprise those who have become accustomed of hearing from the present-day advocates of Christianity that their religion was responsible for the softening of the attitude of the Romans regarding slaves. No, it was not Christianity—that greatest upholder of slavery. Let me quote a Christian writer (Encyclopaedia Britannica, Vol. XXII, p. 134.) :—

"We have observed a change in the policy of the law, indicating a change in the sentiment with respect to slave class, **which does not appear to have been at all due to Christian Teaching,** but to have arisen from the spontaneous influence of circumstances cooperating with the softened manners which were inspired by a pacific regime."

Christianity regenerated the institution of slavery when the Romans were going to abandon it and it used it for centuries in degenerating vast human populations of the world. The description of severities perpetrated by the Christians upon innocent men, women and children of Africa and other countries, to obtain slaves for their colonies, is not pleasant reading. Who can have the courage to deny that the great cities of Christiandom continued to remain the popular slave-markets of the world from the days of Constantine up to 1850 A.D. ? Who among the Christians

1935

MUHAMMAD

THE GLORY OF THE AGES

by

Hafiz Muhammad Fazlurrehman Ansari, B.A.(Alig.)

Member

Jamiat-ush-Shubbanul-Muslimeen, Cairo, Egypt.

Author of :

1936

Appendix 2: Meritorious Achievement

Appendix 3: Comparative Religious Studies

HAFIZ
FAZLUR
REHMAN
ANSARI

B.A., B.Th., JNR.,
ALIGARH.

Reproduced from his book " CHRISTIANITY AT THE CROSSROADS."

"He (i.e., Jesus) is nothing but a servant (of God) on whom We (i.e., God) bestowed favour, and We made him a pattern for the Children of Israel." (Quran, XLIII, 59.)

"He (i.e., Jesus) spake: Lo! I am the slave of God. He hath given me the Scripture and hath appointed me a Prophet,

"And hath made me blessed wheresoever I may be, and hath enjoined upon me prayer and alms-giving so long as I remain alive.

"And hath made me dutiful toward her who bore me, and hath not made me arrogant, unblest.

"Peace on me the day I was born, and the day I die, and the day I shall be raised alive!

"Such was Jesus, son of Mary: (this is) a statement of the truth concerning which they doubt.

"It befitteth not (the Majesty of) God that He should take unto Himself a son, Glory be to Him! When He decreeth a thing, He saith unto it only: Be and it is.

"And lo! God is my Lord and your Lord. So serve Him. That is the right path." (Quran, XIX. 30—36.)

"No heathen tribe had ever conceived so grotesque an idea, involving, as it does, the assumption that man was born with a hereditary stain upon him, that this stain for which he was not personally responsible had to be atoned for, and that the Creator of all things was compelled to make a blood sacrifice of His own innocent son in order. to neutralise this mys= terious curse."—Sir Arthur Conan Doyle ("My Religion," published in "Daily Express," September 12, 1925).

" . . . . positive Christianity has lost its hold on the majority of more highly educated persons, and it is only a question of time before it ceases to retain the allegiance of the majority of Englishmen."—H. G. Woods, Principal of Woodbrooke ("Christian Life," October 23, 1926).

Appendix 4: Eminent Philosophy Scholar and Teacher

<h2>LETTER FROM HAFIZ FAZLUR REHMAN ANSARI, M.A., B.Th. (Hons.)</h2>

Hafiz Fazlur Rehman Ansari, M.A., B.Th.

Muslim Univerversity,
ALIGHAR.
19/8/45.

Some time back you sent a letter to my revered teacher, Professor Dr. Syed Zafar - ul - Hasan, M.A., D.Phil. (Oxon.), Dr.Phil. (Erl.), to write some things for your series of publications. I have got two essays in my hands now you will be very glad to hear. His Exalted Eminence has gone through them and he feels that they must be published soon. They are now in the hands of the typist, and shall be on the way to you very soon. They will cover 16 pages of typed foolscap each. Please be ready to publish them as soon as you receive them.

Yours sincerely,

F. R. ANSARI.

Mr. Mohammed Makki,
98 100 Brickfield Road, Durban.

Appendix 5:   The Roving Ambassador of Peace

ISLAM AND COMMUNISM

LETTER FROM MOULANA ABDUL ALEEM SIDDIQUI, AL-QADERI.

Beit-ul-Ilm,
Meerut City.
18-9-45.

Mr. Mohammed Makki,
98-100 Brickfield Road,
Durban, South Africa.

My dear Makki,

The great service which you are rendering to Islam by the publication of missionary periodicals and magazines is indeed a great achievement, particularly in view of your worries, and is of emulation by others. Your selfless enthusiasm for Islam makes me extremely happy and I congratulate you with all my heart. May the Almighty give you further strength and enable you to render greater services to Islam. Amen!

I congratulate you and your friends, Mr. A. I. Timol and Mr. A. M. Kharsany, on providing Rupees 4,000/ for the preparation of "Islam and Communism." I have, however, received one instalment of Rupees 2,000/ so far.

When the book is published the great and noble assistance which you, your friends and others have rendered in this cause will be duly acknowledged. Please convey my most heartfelt congratulations to both of your above-mentioned friends. May Allah inspire in them greater strength of will to serve Islam and shower on them His choicest blessings. Surely, the opportunity of rendering such service comes only to those whom Allah Himself selects. No greater fortune is conceivable.

Please also convey to Mr. S. M. Paruk my heartfelt thanks for his assistance.

With love,
Yours,
M. A. ALEEM SIDDIQUI.

When the IRO was founded in 1949, its constitution provided that the council would be composed of: Muslims, Protestants, Roman Catholics, Buddhists, Hindus, Confucianists, Sikhs, Jews, and

THE FOUNDER OF MAKKI PUBLICATIONS

Fazlur Rahman Ansari: Life and Thought Abdul Aleem Siddiqui and his Mission

Short Reviews

Abdul Aleem Siddiqui and His Mission. By Abdul Kader Choughley. Durban, South Africa, Ahsan Publications. 2013, ISBN: 978-0-920-58293-3, Pp. 229.

Fazlur Rahman Ansari: Life and Thought. By Abdul Kader Choughley. Durban, South Africa, Ahsan Publications. 2012, ISBN: 97806254784, Pp. 285.

In recent years Abdul Kader Choughley, a South African scholar, has made a mark as the chronicler and analyst of the Islamic intellectual tradition, particularly of the Indo-Pak subcontinent. His area of expertise is Islamic resurgence in 20th century in South Asia. Since Sayyid Abul Hasan Ali Nadwi (1913-1999) prominently figures among the Islamic revivalists in the region, it is not unsurprising that Choughley's earlier works were *Islamic Resurgence: Sayyid Abul Hasan Ali Nadwi and his Contemporaries* (2011) and *Sayyid Abul Hasan Ali Nadwi: Life and Works* (2012). Ahsan Academy, headed by Choughley, has published also the intellectual biography of another leading Islamic scholar, *From Darkness Into Light: Life and Works of Mawlana Abdul Majid Daryabadi (1892-1977)*.

Abdul Aleem Siddiqui (1892-1954) was both an Islamic scholar and *muballigh* (*da'wah* activist) par excellence and a Sufi master in his own right, with a non-sectarian approach. Born in Meerut, India, he turned his attention to *tabligh* (preaching of Islam) before Mawlana Ilyas's trend- setting, global Tablighi Jama`at movement. Siddiqui was thoroughly grounded in Islamic scholarship and adept at English, Arabic, Persian and Urdu. As part of his mission he toured extensively the Arab world, Europe, the Caribbean islands, Singapore and South Africa. Apart from delivering lectures on Islam, he bought out two Islamic magazines, *Genuine Islam* and *Voice of Islam.* As an activist he championed also the cause of the Pakistan movement in 1940s in the Arab world and secured Hasan Al-Banna's help and support for this cause. As early as in 1949 he set up in Singapore the Society for the Promotion of Inter-Religious Cooperation, which engaged major faith leaders Amid his several works, the following deserve special mention: i) *Dimensions of Islam* ii) *The Principles of Islam,* iii) *The Forgotten Path of Knowledge* iv) *A Shavian* and a *Theologian* and v) *Cultivation of Science by Muslims.* His writings in Urdu deal with *sirah*, Sufism and repudiation of Qadianism. Choughley's work succeeds remarkably in unravelling various aspects of Siddiqui's multidimensional personality, especially his religious fervor for promoting Islam and his inspiring works. Another laudable feature of Choughley's work is his cross-referencing, which enables readers to gain fruitful acquaintance with most of the publications on the intellectual history of Islam in the Indo-Pak subcontinent. Choughley is to be complimented for both his lucid presentation and his insightful scholarship.

In his *Fazlur Rahman Ansari: Life and Thought,* Choughley vividly brings into relief the accomplishments of Siddiqui's illustrious disciple, Fazlur Rahman Ansari (1914-1974) who carried further his mentor's mission. Born in 1914 in Muzaffar Nagar, India, Ansari first pursued Dars-i Nizami at Madrasah Islamiyah, and then pursued his, BA, MA. B.Th and Ph.D. in philosophy at the Aligarh Muslim University. It was in 1932 that he first came into contact with Abdul Aleem Siddiqui who initiated him in both Sufism and *Tabligh.* Ansari served as a member of the Education Planning Committee set up by M.

A. Jinnah for the new state of Pakistan. While following in Siddiqui's footsteps, Ansari delivered lectures on Islam in various countries and contributed to Inter-Faith deliberations. The Aleemiyah Institute established by him in Karachi went a long way in honing some bright Muslim scholars. Amid Ansari's several books, the following won a wide acclaim: i) *Foundations of Faith,* ii) *Islam and the Western Civilisation,* iii) *Islam versus Marxism,* iv) *The Quranic Foundations and Structure of Muslim Society* and v) *Through Science and Philosophy to Religion.* Throughout his life long *da'wah* Ansari placed premium on *tawhid* (the concept of the One True God), Sufism anchored deep into the Quran and Sunnah, and Islam as the natural way ensuring the success of man in both the worlds. He exhorted fellow Muslims to internalize the Islamic concept and practice of *islah* (individual and social reform) and *tazkiyah* (self-development and self-purgation). He devoted his considerable time and energy to preaching and consolidating Islam in its pristine purity in South Africa and Seychelles and hence Choughley's glowing tribute to him. For Ansari's invaluable mission led to the Islamic resurgence across the world.

Choughley has done well to document the biography, methodology and achievements of these two laudable Islamic revivalists. It is hoped he will continue this invaluable series both for inspiration and posterity. We look forward to many more such tracts.

Abdur Raheem Kidwai
Aligarh Muslim University, Aligarh India

Source: *The Muslim World Book Review.* Volume 38: 2018, 74-5.

Appendix 7: *The Glorious Qur'an:*
Abdul Majid Daryabadi

I take this opportunity to give the glad tiding that Maulana Abdul Majid of Daryabad (India) is preparing the translation and commentary in English. More than one- third of the work has been completed and it is hoped that, Insha-Allah, it will reach the hands of the public by the year 1937.

(*A New Muslim World in the Making*, 108).

Fazlur Rahman Ansari, a notable Islamic scholar was greatly impressed by Daryabadi's *tafsir*. Both of them studied at the AMU and shared a common academic background in Philosophy, Psychology and Sociology which augmented their respective readings of the Qur'anic moral code. For example, Ansari's citation from Daryabadi's commentary on societal duties illustrates the latter's extensive familiarity with sociological trends. More importantly, Daryabadi's articulation of the Islamic moral code epitomises their unconditional commitment to Islam shorn of the spirituality overload. Overall, a laudable feature of their Qur'anic contributions is their impartial and non-sectarian mindset.

(*Abdul Majid Daryabadi's Tafsir-ul-Qur'an: A Critical Study*, 71-2).

Selected Bibliography

Alladin, Ibrahim, *Maulana Abdul Aleem Siddiqui: His Life, Thoughts and Message* (Curepipe, 2019).

Ansari, Fazlur Rahman, *A New Muslim World in the Making* (Karachi, 2018).

- *Muhammad The Glory of the Ages* (Karachi, 2017).

- *Islam and Christianity in the Modern World* (Karachi, 2017).

- *Communist Challenge to Islam: An Exposition of Communism vis-à-vis Islam* (Karachi, 2018).

- *Through Science and Philosophy to Islam* (Karachi, 1976).

- *Islam versus Marxism* (Karachi, 1982).

- *Islam versus Communism* (Karachi, 1982).

- *The Qur'ānic Foundations and Structure of Muslim Society* (Karachi, 2012).

Asad, Muhammad, *Islam at the Crossroads* (Lahore, 1969).

Choughley, Abdul Kader, *Abdul Aleem Siddiqui and his Mission* (Springs, 2013).

Fazlur Rahman Ansari: Life and Thought (Springs, 2012).

Ghazali, Muhammad, *The Socio-Political Thought of Shah*

WaliAllah (Islamabad, 2001).

Gupta, Juhi and Kidwai, Abdur Raheem (editors), *Oxford of the East: Aligarh Muslim University 1920-2020* (New Delhi, 2020).

Hasan, Syed Zafarul, *Why Religion* (Karachi, 1976).

Iqbal, Muhammad, *The Reconstruction of Religious Thought in Islam* (Lahore, 1971).

Khan, Muhammad Mojlum, *Great Muslims of the West: Makers of Western Islam* (Leicester, 2017).

Khalil, Rāna, *Tadhkirah 'Allāmah Fazlur Rahman Ansari Al-Qādri* (Lahore,1992).

Kidwai, Abdur Raheem, *Translating the Untranslatable* (New Delhi, 2011).

Kidwai, Abdur Raheem (ed.), *Sir Syed Ahmad Khan: Renaissance Man of India* (New Delhi, 2017).

Kriel, Mahdie, *Intellectual Islamic Revival of the Modern Mind* (Cape Town, 2011).

Mohamed, Yasien, *Islam to the Modern Mind* (Paarl, 2006).

Muhammad Yahya, Abu Abdul Quddus, *Uhd i-Sāz Shakhsiyyat: Hāidh Dr Fazlur Rahman Al-Ansāri Al-Qādri* (Karachi, 2018).

Nadwi, Abul Hasan Ali, *Western Civilisation, Islam and Muslims* (Lucknow, 1974).

- *Purrn i-Charrgh*, vol.1 (Karachi, 1984).

- *Purrn i-Charrgh*, vol. 2 (Karachi, 1981).

- *Rise and Fall of Muslims; Its Impact on the World* (Springs, 2020).

Nizami, Khaliq Ahmad, *History of Aligarh Muslim University* (Delhi, 1995).

Robinson, Francis, *The 'Ulama of Farang Mahall and Islamic Culture in South Asia* (Delhi, 2000).

Siddiqui, Abdul Aleem, *Dimensions of Islam* (Durban, 2008).

Siddiqui, Umair Mahmood, *The Beacon Light* (Karachi, 2015).

- *Maktubāt i-Ansari* (Karachi, 2018).

Zaman, Muhammad Qasim, *The 'Ulama in Contemporary Islam: Custodians of Change* (Princeton. 2002).